PRINTHOUSE BOOKS PRESENTS

Cursed by the Candy
Drama & Suspense

KaToi Love
VIP INK Publishing Group, Inc.
Atlanta, GA.

KaToi Love

©KaToi Love 2016
PrintHouse Books, Atlanta, GA.
Published 6 - 15 -2016
www.PrintHouseBooks.com

VIP INK Publishing Group; Incorporated

All rights reserved. No parts of this book may be reproduced in any way, shape, or form or by any means without permission in writing from the publisher, or the author, except by a reviewer.

Cursed by the Candy

Cover art, designed by Gifted Group llc.
ISBN: 978-1-5323-0349-4

Library of Congress Cataloging-in-Publication Data

KaToi Love

Cursed by the Candy

1. Drama 2.Romance 3.Crime 4.Urban Literature 5. KaToi Love

KaToi Love

Dedication

This book is dedicated to all the young women who believe that money can buy their Soul.

This book is dedicated to the girl who was afraid to be loved.

This book is dedicated to my Mother who would scream every time I shared a chapter from my book.

This book is dedicated to my Father who has always encouraged and loved me.

This book is dedicated to the life I was blessed to bring into this world my children Deja and Kienon.

This book is dedicated to my heart that skips a beat when I think about the man who inspired this book.... the REAL PJ.

I would be nothing without the gift of GOD, my Lord and Savior who created me with this craft.

Thank you in Jesus name .... Amen

Synopsis

"Cursed by the Candy "is an urban love tale. Toi's existence revolved around the materials only a hustler could provide. Money, cars and status were a necessity in order to even approach her. Come correct or don't come at all, that was her philosophy .The avenues she traveled, presented her with life learning experiences. The "candy" was sweet, however the consequences weren't. Money was her motivation, but love took her soul. PJ introduced her to the game, but D is why she played it.

Follow Toi's journey down to "Candy" Land and ask yourself ...was it worth it?

KaToi Love

KaToi Love

Cursed by the Candy

Drama & Suspense

**VIP INK Publishing Group,
Incorporated**

Atlanta, GA

Cursed by the Candy

Table of Contents

Introduction: *Cursed by the Candy*	8
Chapter 1	9
Chapter 2	65
Chapter 3	96
Chapter 4	137
Chapter 5	273
Chapter 6	316
Chapter 7	338
Chapter 8	376
Chapter 9	395

KaToi Love

Cursed by the Candy

My life was made evil by the materials of man, if you haven't lived my life you wouldn't understand.

I was possessed by a drug that is hard to explain. It made crack or heroine seem like child's play.

The drug was called "Candy" the sugar of man, I overdosed on its sweetness, and it grabbed me when I ran.

It entered my veins with such a push, my soul became inflamed by its sugar rush.

This drug made me weak, like I had been cursed with the worse disease, by the time I realized what happened I dropped to my knees. I begged God to help me, detox me in a way that the candy couldn't influence me another day.

Cursed by the Candy

Chapter One

Why are my eyes always attracted to the dough?-- Ballers and hustlers whatever you may call them. Let me explain this to ya. If you don't rock a nice whip, have phat grip don't step to me. I know you're probably thinking, how shallow can you be? Well, the way I figure it, nothing's for free; this has always been my problem. Where it came from, I don't know, but I do believe it's a curse.

My mind or body will not react to anything less than the "candy. "Yes, I said "Candy." Something that looks so sweet you can just taste it in your soul. This has always been an issue and will probably be 'til the day the good Lord places me in the ground.

KaToi Love

I was never what you may call a statistic. I wasn't poor, didn't grow up in the hood and was never sexually abused. The type of issues that may cause your mind to come up with the drama my life has been surrounded by.

Look here, Toi was adored from the day I arrived from my momma's "canal of love". I call it that because my daddy loved every inch of Chanelle and I was definitely a product of that love. Unfortunately God needed another angel and took my daddy when I was only five. Still I remember him as if it were just yesterday. Chilling on the couch with those big headphones listening to Earth Wind and Fire and bopping his head; yes, my daddy loved his music, and next to me and Chanelle, music was his heart and soul.

Cursed by the Candy

I was adored from the start and if Momma and Daddy felt that way any man coming in my direction better represent.

See, the way I figure it is we ladies fall short sometimes letting a brotha control us, but why? We have what they want, the jewels between or thighs. Look I am hardly a whore, but respect thyself: mind, body and pockets.

All my friends call me Toi, but my government name is ShaToia, yeah moms was tripping, don't act like your name is not a little questionable "Mercedes" yes, we all have fallen victim to the ghetto-fabulous names. Ladies we all know I speak the truth and I am dead serious when I talk about the "candy" it should be treated with the

KaToi Love

utmost respect. Let's keep it real ...Toi cannot eat or sleep without dreaming of $$$$$$. I realize, by not studying the game, you can be converted from Diva to Chickenhead in a matter of a second, but not me because I have a plan. Know how to play your position and don't find yourself in the wrong one.

I swear I was in a trance by the candy so much that it blinded all my senses .I could not hear, feel, smell or see without the sweetness, and that's when the curse kicked in.

Why do people ask, 'where are you from'? Where you are from is a state of mind. Hell, I'm from Chanelle.

I was brought up here and there so I never classified myself as far as being

Cursed by the Candy

from one particular place, however if I had to narrow it down though, Boston, Virginia and North Carolina are my most memorable memories.

These places are where Ms. Toi learned, that everything that sweet is hardly good for ya.

~~~~~

It's 2 o'clock in the morning and I am half dead from the pool party my brother had after school, never mind the fact that I have been up all evening trying to do my homework, so maybe I can pass to the next grade.

Chanelle keeps yelling up the stairs like a crazy woman. My momma, love her to death, but at this particular moment she is really pissing me off. I roll off the bed and make it to the door, "Yeah ma." I answer, trying to get up before she makes it to the top of the stairs, then I know it's on.

There's silence for a moment and then I hear her saying, "Why the hell are these dishes still in the sink?"

As I roll my eye's and walk back to my bed, I start thinking Toi you better stop tripping. I jump up quick, because Chanelle does not play. See my momma is about 5'4", 125-- a bangin' body and what I would call a 'Diva Workaholic'. She works 18 hour days, but looking at her you would think she just walked off of a runway.

Cursed by the Candy

Chanelle introduced me to the "candy "at the early age of 15. Momma had two hair salons and she worked the hell out of them. If you lived in Boston in the late 80s you knew Ms. Chanelle, and if you didn't you wanted to. Short hair, long hair, no hair-- it didn't matter, if you had 100 dollars or more, Chanelle would hook you up.

Momma worked the craziest hours so parental supervision was unheard of in my house. Don't feel bad, though I was hardly lacking love, Chanelle provided me with all I needed.

My friends were called Filenes, Macy's and Niemen Marcus. Momma may not have had a lot of time, but she showered me with the "candy" always. Emotional love would have to be found elsewhere.

Chanelle worked here fingers to the bone, Monday through Saturday, but on Sunday it was on. Watch out Neiman Marcus here we come. Now Saturday's I had to prepare for our weekend shopping sprees. My hair was always tight due to her occupation; Gloria Vanderbilt jeans tight and fitting right, my body was soft and shoes where straight off the showroom floor.

I am only 16, but the way I'm shaped you would think I was at least 18 or maybe 19. My family must have the best genes ever and I swear I have inherited all of them. I'm 5'5", 105, nice round ass and small but perky breasts. However, I'm confident that will improve in time .Call me conceded or whatever, I am just confident. No low self esteem running over here.

Cursed by the Candy

Hell, I figure work with what you got. Saturday morning comes around and I am more than ready. I may be sharing the mall with moms, but this doesn't mean my radar is not in full effect. Ladies always be on the look out for the "Candy man" no matter what the circumstance is....except church, that's just straight wrong.

~~~~~

This particular day the mall was crowded as hell, and after about 5 hours of shopping, I was tired and ready to roll out. Looking at Chanelle you would have never known we had been in here forever-- she was running around here like the damn energizer bunny. Passing cards out, talking to everybody that came around with a torn up hairdo.

Talk about taking networking to another level... I'm ready to go. I sat there looking around all crazy, wishing I could take these expensive ass shoes off. Then I glanced over and saw Chanelle giving me that evil mamma look and I decided to chill. I don't know what it is about parents, but they have this weird sense when their offspring is tripping and Chanelle had it like the Bionic Woman. I sat there rubbing my feet because I could swear they were bleeding and that's when I saw him.

My eye's eye began to get glassy and I thought *who in the world is that?* This was my first encounter with PJ and in my heart I knew it would not be the last. Let me tell you, in my mind this brotha was floating across the store like an angel-- he was brown skinned, had

Cursed by the Candy

wavy hair and was rocking a black Karl Kani outfit; he had on a gold rope chain that was all that to finish it off. I had to blink twice to make sure I wasn't dreaming. Now I am hardly shy, but he had me feeling all silly and young-- let's keep it real, shit, who am I trying to fool, I am young.

I looked around and Chanelle was out of sight; I had to take this opportunity to talk to home boy. I pulled my compact out to freshen up my lips and there she was. I could see her through the mirror.

I stood up and approached her slowly. "Ma, I need to go to the bathroom, I'll be right back".

She turned around and said" Toi you think I'm stupid? I see your fast ass over there, sit down somewhere."

I took a step back to make sure no one could hear her; man, she so embarrassing sometimes. I thought I would try one last time and pray I didn't get smacked.

"No ma, I really need to go to the bathroom."

I pleaded a bit more and finally she agreed," Go ahead girl."

I turned and walked away and I could feel her staring me down-- I thought about turning around, but decided to keep it moving. I began to scan the store like I was in search of a shoplifter, but I was looking for someone who could lift up my stock.

The nerves in my body were shot. I turned the corner and there he was, looking at some fly ass shoes. I walked in his direction and said, "Excuse me, would you like a card to my mom's hair salon? You can get your Shorty's hair hooked up."

He took the card from my hand and looked at it; I was so nervous I felt like I was sweating all over. He removed his eyes from the card and said, "Thank you."

I gave him a fake smirk and began to walk away. He cleared his throat and I felt a nudge on my arm. He licked his lips and stared in my eyes and said, "Maybe I'll do that".

Stepping was the only thing on my mind; at this point I could barely breath…..*Calm down Toi, calm down Toi* is all I was saying.

I left the mall that day, and felt different for some reason. I could tell that things were about to change. But who would have known how much.

~~~~~

Saturday rolled around and I could not stop thinking about this stranger I met the other day. I woke up, did my daily weekend thing and then remembered I was at the shop all day…*Damn*. I looked in the mirror and wondered where I would be ten years from now. *Would I have a degree* ?-- Well at this rate probably not. *Would I have a family or just be alone?* I sat back on the bed and stared at the wall. I sat there for a minute until my thoughts were interrupted by a loud bang!

I jumped off the bed and ran into the hall, "What was that?"

I turned the corner and saw this girl sitting on the steps laughing. I looked down and saw my clown-ass brother helping her up.

"Boy if you don't get that girl out of here Chanelle is going to kill you!"

Mike looked up and said, "Mind your business Toi…"

Then I replied, "This is my business stupid! I am going to be the one who has to hear her mouth all day long."

I started getting irritated because this chick was still laughing. I looked at her retarded ass and said, "Let's see how funny this is when my momma whips your ass… stupid."

I walked away and began to get ready for the day. Anybody who has ever been to a hair salon knows that's the place to be on a Saturday, and for as long as I can remember, I was there. Chanelle had me washing hair, taking out weave, sweeping the floor.

I swear this had to be the longest ride. Chanelle fussed all the way about my dumb brother. I knew this would happen, and he had the nerve to tell me to mind my business. I pretended to listen to her, but my thoughts were a thousand miles away.

Finally we got to the shop and I started my weekend ritual. Towels washed, sweeping the floor—blah, blah, blah. All of a sudden everyone seemed to be distracted; I turned my head around to see what was causing the commotion, and right there he stood. He was stepping out of a royal blue 325I BMW walking towards my momma's shop.

My heart dropped and I ran and looked in the mirror real quick; I made my way back to the front and looked out the window. Since I am also the receptionist, Chanelle was not too pressed about me talking to this man. He walked into the shop and chimes rang on the door, "Can I help you?" I asked.

He looked at me and licked his lips and said," You told me if I wanted to get my girl's hair done this was the place to come."

My head started spinning and, I thought some chick was about to stroll through the door, he must have seen the disappointment in my face because he said, "I decided to come by and hook you up Shorty."

I looked at him like he had lost his mind,, but this brotha's expression was dead serious.

Everybody's eyes were all on my back; I turned around and Chanelle was grilling me hard-- *Please don't embarrass me up in here.* I gave him a look like this is not the time; he caught on quick and acted like he was making an appointment. He put his number down with the quickness and left.

I thought to myself, *Please let this day end so I can get home and call him.* Soon as I got through the door I was on the phone in a micro second. My heart was about to thump out of my chest. *Lawd, don't let me have a heart attack up here.* I needed a drink bad. I had some private stock under my bed, if my nosey ass brother didn't find it.

I walked over to my dresser and turned on the radio, maybe it would calm my nerves. I started screaming when I heard my song "I'll give all my love" by Keith Sweat. That's all I needed to put me in the mood. I pulled a piece of paper out of my pocket and brought it to my nose. Damn it smelled just like him...*ummmmm*. I sat down and grabbed the phone and as the phone began to ring I realized I didn't even know his name. As I was about to hang up I heard a deep sexy voice.

"Hello," he said.

I didn't know what to say, but I did recognize his voice. I started to speak and then all the nerves went away.

"Hey this is Toi, from the hair salon."

He started to giggle and said, "What's up, Shorty."

I paused for a moment then said, "You forgot to give me your name."

He laughed and said, "You didn't ask.

I saw he was trying to be a smart ass so I said, "I'm asking now." He paused for a moment then said, "My name is PJ." -- After all of the formalities were established, he said, "You look kind of young to be on the phone so late."

I paused for a moment to let his comment sink in and said to myself, *Let me handle this.* All of the noise in the back ground was starting to wear on my nerves. PJ sighed and said, "Oh, I have Miss Attitude on the phone? So what's up with you for tonight?"

I looked at the clock and thought to myself *What the hell does he think, it's damn near midnight.* I responded, "Nothing, just getting home from work. What about you?"

The soft sound of his voice had me mesmerized and he knew it. After about another five minutes of conversation he said, "I'm in route to pick something up from my boy."

His word sunk in and I said, "You're in the car?"

"Yeah I'm driving now."

Damn he has a phone in his car; now Chanelle makes a grip and she doesn't even have a car phone. My mind started wondering off and I began to become embarrassed, he must think I am some kind of clown. I'm a firm believer in a first impression and right about now I was coming off as a fool, but, dang, give me a break I was new at this.

PJ softly said "Can you get out tonight?"

I knew I should have said no. Chanelle would kill me if she knew I was about to leave out her house at midnight, but what the hell, you only live once and I planned on living it up, "Yeah."

I gave him the directions to my house and went to check on moms. I hoped she was knocked out for the night, and was just as I thought, sleeping like a baby.

Something in my head is always trying to change my mind. I guess it's my conscience. I heard it loud and clear at this point, *Toi, what are you doing?"*

~~~~~

PJ picked me up that night and we have been inseparable for the past two months. I am no longer the shy girl he met in the mall; now I'm his girl.

Cursed by the Candy

It's not hard to spend time with him. Chanelle is never home so we have dinner together every night and he is the last face I see before I go to sleep. After hanging out with PJ 24/7, I certainly realize why he can afford such extravagant items. PJ is a hustler and I should have realized that from day one, but to be honest with you all it has really done is turn me on more.

My baby picks me up from school every day like clock work; he is really doing his thing. The moment I step out of the building I see him across the street chilling waiting for me to approach. It's so funny to me because I see all the tricks checking him out, shit look-- but at the end of the day he's mine.

I was never the type of chick to deal with a lot of bitches, but sometimes you need a little female companionship, like when I want to brag about how my boo takes me shopping every week; but hell ,I don't have to brag...it's obvious .

Don't get me wrong, I'm hardly broke down by any means, but now my clothes have mad flava. Diamond earrings, bracelets with my name engraved in them. I swear I have about 20 pairs of sneakers and shoes.

My momma thinks I've lost my mind because I never want to go shopping. Hiding everything is beginning to be a problem; she would have a damn conniption if she saw this stuff. See I have been thinking about this entire relationship thing and I have come up with a theory, PJ is sprung, that's what I call it.

I am still holding on to the jewels. Sex is something I have never experienced. That makes me a prize in his eyes; my baby says that's one of the things he adores about me, I have never shared myself with anyone before. Now don't get it twisted I know he has bitches flocking around him like flies to shit, but that comes with the territory .We see each other every day and he takes care of me lovely. Respect, that's important, no it's required, in order to roll with Toi.

~~~~~

Ladies never get too comfortable; I should have been on his ass like a bear to her cubs. I knew this mess wouldn't last forever. Keith Sweat says, "Make it last Forever". Dang PJ, could we have made it last for three months without some bullshit?

I looked at my watch and start fuming; I've been standing out here, mind you for 20 minutes, looking dumb as shit. PJ still hasn't picked me up. I try and calm down, *Toi don't let these hoes see you out here sweating over no man.* Tonya comes out and looks directly my way. Now, of all days for my rival to be out here-- She approaches me and says "What's up baby, got stood up?"

I turned around knowing that my ears had to be playing tricks on me. I know this bitch didn't just say something .The frustration I was feeling for PJ came out and Tonya was my prey. I smacked her so hard I broke a nail. Fuck all the small talk, who the hell does she think she's trying to embarrass?

Tonya was so shocked, she didn't know what to do .PJ's loud ass music brought me back to my senses. He got out all smooth while I'm standing they're with my hair all messed up.

He walks in my direction and had the nerve to say "Boo, what's up?"

I looked at him and rolled my eyes and walked towards the car. The moment we pulled off I said, "What took you so long?" PJ didn't answer, so I asked him again. This time he smacked me in the face.

I'll never forget the look on his face. Still to this day his eyes reminded me of the devil. He turned his head and said, "Don't ever raise your voice at me, Toi?"

I sat there in disbelief; I don't know if I was scared to death or hurt, but I sure the hell was confused.

I sat there and decided being quiet was the best bet for me now. Besides I didn't know what to say. *I can't believe he just smacked me in the face.* PJ dropped me off and I haven't spoken with him since.

~~~~~

I keep telling my self it's for the best, but my heart doesn't agree keeping my chatter at a constant, "Oh God, I feel so sick."

I've been calling him and he won't answer his phone. I waited outside a couple of days, and he never came.

I sat on my bed wondering, *Baby, why are you doing this to me?* I sobbed uncontrollably in my pillow. Seven days had passed and I was through. Eating was out of the question and I definitely couldn't sleep. All I could do was think about PJ.

Chanelle said she was going to take me to the doctor if I didn't get my shit together.

~~~~~

I sat there in the dark wondering if anyone would miss me if I was gone....*probably not*, I thought. I rolled over and looked at the red lights on the clock and it read 12:03-- as I started to dose off the phone rang. I reached over and grabbed it before Chanelle did. In a groggy voice I said, "Hello?" All I could hear was loud music playing, Eric B and Rakim in the background. "Hello??" I said. Then that familiar voice took over the phone line.

It was PJ.

He paused then said "Toi, I bet you won't raise your voice again."

I didn't even respond, I was just so happy to hear his voice.

"Put your clothes on, I'll pick you up in a minute." I headed to the bathroom and washed up.

That night I gave PJ my sweetness. I had never done this before, but my body took over. He was very gentle and showed me how much he missed me. We talked about the way things took place and PJ promised to never raise his hand at me again. I promised to always play my position. People always have good intentions when promises are made, but deep down we know they'll be broken.

Ladies, being a hustler's girl is a full-time job. Never disrespect your man, always keep your mouth shut and fuck all the other bitches.

Me and PJ were back on track again, or so I thought.

As I strolled down the hall like I owned the world I noticed Tonya and her flunky's staring at me. I pause for a moment and look them dead in their faces. These chicks think since I pretty much keep to myself and say as few words as possible I must be a punk or something.

Let me set the record straight, Ms. Toi is hardly soft, but I choose my battles, I don't let them choose me. I refuse to get caught up in romper room type of behavior.

Ladies, please explain to me why we as females always hate on one another? -- So much energy being wasted on the bullshit. I, for example, focus my energy on other things such as, what am I going to wear to school day by day to make these chicks really hate on me and due to the fact that I don't keep much company, I come up with ways to entertain myself. While their getting all pissed that their boyfriends are looking my way, I just sit back like it's a movie and laugh.

This is the way I figure it, if you are not putting cream in my pockets, buying my clothes or feeding me, you really don't matter. See I give props where props are due. If I see a female with a nice outfit on, I'll be the first to throw out a compliment. Low self esteem is hardly my problem .No chick is as fly as me, and if for some reason you are, do your thing girl. You would be an asset, shit, two Divas are better then one anyway. We could be a team, compliment each other's flyness. Unfortunately, the female society doesn't share my views on this. They would rather be haters and keep the drama stirring. This is why I fly solo-- me, me and me.

Let me school you on the whole Tonya story. For some reason this chick has always been a hater, always saying little sarcastic things about my hair or my eyes. These are my best assets, so I figure she is just jealous. No let me rephrase this... I know she is. God blessed me with eyes like a cat and hair down my back. I find all of this extremely amusing though. I would always reply to her remarks with, "I sure do have a weave boo-boo, you want my momma to hook you up?"

This only infuriates her, so my goal has been reached. I just flipped it on her dumb ass and to add fire to the flame, her ragged little boyfriend keeps sending me flowers and writing me these stupid love letters. Which has really caused home girl to trip, but as I sit down and think about it, it's all really just sad. Tonya is a nice looking girl, but she just uses too much energy on the nonsense. Now if she was smart and calmed down a few notches, I would even consider befriending her. You know, help her to enhance her assets .Who am I fooling though, you know that will never happen. Haters keep hating on, while Toi keeps moving on.

Life has been wonderful since me and PJ made up, we have been at it like rabbits, daily my skills have gotten better and I know it. I'm so glad Chanelle is working late tonight. I have it all planned out, just me and my baby. I've been reading a lot lately, trying to get some pointers on the whole romance thing. I plan on keeping my man. Candles, wine and lingerie, it's going to be on tonight.

I just need to make sure my brother doesn't decide to make an appearance.

As I'm sitting there staring at the clock waiting for 3oclock to hit, I really start thinking about how much I hate school I could be doing something else easily. I watch the arms go around the clock and I start counting down, four more minutes then I'm out of here.

Cursed by the Candy

The bell finally rings and I get up with finesse. Straight to the bathroom I go, need to make sure everything is in place. Always look good for your man, or someone else will. First thing I hear when I approach the door is gossiping. I'm so not in the mood for Tonya and her little mob.

I make my way to the mirror, and in my sweetest tone I say, "Excuse me ladies." Tonya turns around and grits on me real hard.

"No, you're not excused."

I smile at her and say, "Look, I don't have time for your tantrums today, my man is outside waiting on me, maybe you can take some notes, so your man will stay out of my face. In fact boo, here's a letter he wrote me today."

I hand it to her, but she drops it on the ground. I start laughing and say, "Don't be mad, you're obviously not handling your business."

I stepped around her and went to meet PJ. My lips are on fire thinking about seeing him. I got in the car and laid the fattest kiss on him. He smiled and said, "Damn girl, you must have really missed me. I need to stay gone more often."

I replied, "No you don't".

I rubbed my hand across his cheek and looked into his eyes; he touched my hand softly and said, "Toi don't be mad, I have some business to take care of tonight. I don't know how long it's going to take."

I felt my throat close up and I turned and faced the window. It took all I had not to question him, but you know my rule, never question your man.

PJ grabs my chin and says "Baby don't be upset. I have to make that dough so you can have nice things like this." He pulls a box out of his pocket, there lays a 3-carat diamond studded necklace. He looks at me and says "You still mad?"

Now ladies you know diamonds are a girl's best friend. I put my arms around him and whisper," I just miss you baby."

PJ drops me off, and I start feeling a bit depressed. There's no need for me to sit around here looking all dumb. I go in the kitchen and whip up a fat lobster, steak and potato, and eat my worries away.

I turn around when I here the door open and look who decides to make an appearance today-- my other half, Mike. I swear he gets on my nerves to the end of this earth, however, I love him. He's about 6'2", dark skinned, waves so deep you would easily get seasick. I must admit my brother is fine.

Mike comes in and says," What's up, Toi?"

"Nothing," I replied.

"Where have you been this week and last?"

"Right here, where yo' ass been?"

Mike replies, "Chilling, anyone call me?"

"Yeah, a couple of your freaks keep calling every ten minutes. I guess they figure if they keep calling you will magically appear or something. You need to get your own phone line. What I look like, your secretary?"

Mike laughs and says, "Shut up! What's your problem? PJ got my sis all pissed off?"

I turn and walk towards the stairs and say, "Oh yeah, Chanelle said call her at the shop."

Me and my Mike have this sibling rivalry going. I'm 15 and Mike is 19; he swears that I run my mouth too much, always getting him in trouble, but I view it totally different. Mike gets himself in trouble. Trying to be a hustler and from the suburbs.

Chanelle takes good care of us; we don't want or need for anything. Momma would have a cow if she knew her only son was out here trying to sell some stupid drugs always out at the projects. Never mind the nasty ass hoes he messes with, trying to make him their next baby daddy. Oh, hell yeah, I'm going to tell! Those sheezas won't be up in here, no Auntie Toi coming out of their mouths, never that. Don't get it twisted though, if one of those chicks come at my brother wrong, I will lay some whip ass on them quick. Don't mess with my family.

I get upstairs and lay across the bed, dang I didn't realize I was so tired; as I start to daydream about the night I thought me and PJ was about to have, the phone rings.

I slowly roll over and search for the phone, through my irritation I say, "Hello."

I hear a soft voice on the other end and immediately get a smile on my face, "What's up baby, why you sounding all evil, you sleep or something?"

Running my hands over my head I slowly say "Hey girl, what's up?"

Sharice says, "Nothing, just thinking about my favorite cousin."

I grin and say, "That's sweet, I needed that girl."

Sharice's voice begins to rise and she says, "Guess what? My mom said Chanelle's been talking about moving to Virginia."

My heart began racing and I say, "WHAT?!? No she didn't!" Sharice can be a little extra so I had to take her words with a grain of salt. I started talking slowly and said, "Girl, Chanelle always says stuff like that when she gets pissed off, she isn't moving anywhere."

I could hear Sharice chewing in the phone and then she finally said, "Okay if that's what you want to believe, but I think she may be for real this time, Toi." I couldn't believe what I was hearing, my mind started spinning ...*oh my goodness I can't leave PJ is she crazy!?*

Tears started running down my face and I said, "Riccy I will call you back. "

I walked over to my window and stared at the sky, "God please don't make me leave," I pleaded. My legs became weak and I slid down to the floor. I sat there pondering over the possibility of us actually moving to VA, depression was definitely the road I was about to visit.

Just as I was about to go down the road of self pity Mike called me, "Toi, PJ is downstairs."

I wiped my hands across my face and stood up slowly; how was I ever going to gather the strength to tell PJ this, if it was true? I yelled back at Mike and told him to tell my baby I would be there in a minute. As I looked in the mirror I started wondering why PJ was here anyway.

I made my way down the stairs to hold my baby tight, the thought of this possibly being the end was too much for me to bear. Everything I was feeling disappeared when I saw my man standing at the bottom of the stairs.

I walked past Mike and threw my arms around PJ's neck. I could feel my brother staring me down so I turned around and gave him the finger; he gave it back in return.

Mike disappeared for a second then returned and said," I'm about to step out for a while." Mike walked out the door and my body took on a life of its own.

I pushed PJ up against the wall and held on to him tight, we feel against the railing, and started kissing each other real hard. He sat down on the steps, and I took my clothes off real slow. The excitement took over while his love was waiting for some attention.

I straddled my man like a horse and we made love hard and with purpose. PJ's body started to tense up and then exploded inside me, the room was spinning and my body was limp, that's when I heard keys in the door.

I jumped up real quick and tried to put on my pants, that's when Mike opened the door and a blank stare came over his face. I looked at him with disgust, and he started laughing and went up the stairs.

PJ grabbed my hand and lead me into the living room; I sat on the couch and attempted to get things started again, but he pulled me close and said, "Toi I have to go to New York for a week, I'm rolling out tomorrow."

The expression on my face said everything my mouth wouldn't; he kissed me on the head and said, "Let me run to the car for a minute."

I watched him walk out the door and I felt sick to my stomach. This had to be the worst day ever, not only did my cuz tell me I might be moving, but my crazy ass brother probably will be black mailing me about what he caught us doing.

I heard the door open back up and I pretended to be looking at TV. PJ turned the TV off and said, "Toi, I need you to hold something for me, he pulled out a fat envelope and opened it up, inside was three fake ID's, a wad of money and three birth certificates.

I opened my mouth to ask him what was going on, then I remembered, *play your position.*

He looked at me sternly and said, "Toi, I'm trusting you; don't let no one know you have this shit, this is mad important. If anything ever happens to me, like I get locked up or something, I need you to use this and take care of it …whatever it is. Baby this is not for shopping, getting your nails done or anything like that, you hear me?"

I reached for his hand and said, "I understand." At this point I was speechless so I pulled him into my arms.

PJ started laughing and said, "Damn girl you act like a nigga about to die or something-- chill out."

Cursed by the Candy

I wasn't acting, my heartfelt heavy and my body was numb...something just didn't feel right.

~~~~~

PJ left my house that night and I haven't heard from him since; it's now been two weeks.

Time has been going by so slowly; you never realize how someone is a part of your life until they are gone. Nothing has mattered over the last week or so. I've ditched school three days, can't eat, sleep or anything. I just stare at the phone, praying that my baby will call.

My door flies open and Mike scares the crap out of me. He stands in the doorway and says, "Toi, Lil Rome is downstairs; he said he needs to talk to you."

I look at him like he's crazy and say, "Who is Lil Rome?"

Mike shrugs his shoulders and says, "one of your crazy ass boy's friends."

I sit there searching through my brain for that name ....*Lil Rome...Lil Rome,* that name just didn't sound familiar. My mind went blank as I walked down the hall. I just kept saying please don't tell me something happened to PJ.I opened the door and went out on the porch, I immediately felt uncomfortable when I saw this guy.

Cursed by the Candy

Lil Rome had this long scar on the side of his face and his clothes looked worn down and old. This dude invaded my personal space, he was all in my face talking about, "Can we talk somewhere else, Shorty?"

I wanted to say hell no, but I needed to know what happened to PJ. I began walking down the driveway and he followed, he put his hands in his pockets and began to speak, "Toi, PJ got caught up in New York, and told me that you would know what to do."

I looked at this man like he was an alien; finally the words released from my mouth, "What do you mean caught up?" I knew exactly what he was talking about, but I wanted to hear it from his mouth.

Lil Rome started moving all around and began to look suspicious, he cut his eyes at me then said," The police picked him up and it doesn't look good."

I started thinking about me and PJ's last conversation and started wishing I would have asked some questions instead of playing my position; one thing I did remember is that PJ was insistent about me not saying anything to anyone. I got myself together, and told Lil Rome, "Ok". I turned around and walked back down the driveway.

When I got back into the house, I felt like I was about to collapse.

Chapter Two

The house was dark and my mind was too; all I could think of *was what am I supposed to do?* PJ had trusted me and I wasn't going to let him down. I ran and got the phonebook and looked up, New York City Precinct, and began to dial the numbers. My hands were shaking so bad I had to dial three times before it went through.

I looked up and saw my brother standing in the breezeway. He turned on the TV and said," What's wrong with you?"

The look on my face said it all, I wanted to tell him, but I was so scared. I put the phone down and said, "Nothing."

KaToi Love

Mike flipped through the channels and said, "Toi, you might as well tell me the truth, I already know, everybody does."

"PJ got popped in New York." I sat there and the tears started falling; through my sobs I said," If you already knew, what the hell you asking me for?"

Mike glanced at me with real sincere eyes and said, "I thought you might need some help."

I rolled my eyes and said sarcastically, "What do I have to do to get the devil to help me out?"

Mike stood up and walked towards the door, he stopped and said," Toi you hard on a brother, I was just trying to make sure my sister wasn't about to do something stupid." I picked up the remote and turned the TV off, I just needed to focus. Mike walked out the room and I called the jail.

A husky sounding man answered the phone," New York City Precinct." I tried to speak, but the words would not come out of my mouth, I held my breath and let the words flow, "I'm calling to get some information on a Pondre Jackson."

The man paused then said, "Hold a moment". It seemed like hours before he returned back to the phone, finally the officer said, "Mr. Jackson is being held for trafficking a controlled substance with the intent to distribute. His bail has been set at $250,000."

I could hear his voice, but could not believe the words; the phone dropped out of my hand and I lay on the floor until I heard the beep, beep sound of the dial tone.

I rubbed my hands across the rough musty rug and screamed as loud as I could, "Why did he give me this responsibility!?"

My room was dark and cold just like my spirit; I knelt down under the bed and pulled out the money. One hundred thousand later, I was finished. Never in my life had I been in the room with this much money-- Chanelle had a stash, but nothing like this.

Who was I trying to fool; I would never be able to bail PJ out alone, shit I'm only

16 and you have to be at least 18 or 21 to bail someone out.

I thought about what my brother said and decided to ask him for help. Slowly I walked down the hall and saw Mike in his room; he looked up from his video game and said, "Oh, you need my help now?" I hated to admit it, but I did; he was so smug, he didn't even look my way, he just said, "What do you need, Toi?"

I stood there playing with my hair, and then I finally said, "Can you drive me to New York, to bail PJ out? I'll give you $500.00."

Mike glanced away from the screen for a moment and said, "I'll think about it."

My blood started boiling, but I had no choice but to play this game with him. I started to walk out then turned back around and said, "What is there to think about, you either are going to help me, or you're not."

I must have started to get on his nerves, because he threw the remote down and said, "Look Toi, you came in here asking me for help, you need to chill."

I walked away and slammed the door behind me; I made my way to the bathroom, and turned on the water to calm my nerves. By the time I got out, Mike had made up his mind. I had already known what he was going to do anyway. The moment I gave him the money, his mind was already made up.

Cursed by the Candy

I sat in my brother's Volvo that night and thought about all kinds of things, like: *Did PJ know how scared I was? What, would Chanelle do if she knew what was going on?* -- Who am kidding I already knew that. I pressed my face against the window and felt a chill roll down my spine. The silence of the ride was killing me, so I decided to talk to Mike.

I turned around and asked my brother, "Do you think I'm stupid for going down here to get him out?"

Mike cleared his throat and said, "Toi, does it really matter what I think? You going to do what you want anyway, you must be trying to clear your own mind. "

We got to New York around 8 o'clock in the morning, and as soon as we crossed the state line, I was scared to death. Mike gets on my nerves, but I would never want to get him in trouble, besides, Chanelle would murder me for involving her son in this mess.

My hands started sweating and I was thinking, what if they ask him where the money came from, or how we know PJ? Shit, maybe I need to think about this some more. I turned around with a tremble in my voice and said "Mike, are you ok with this?"

"Yeah… why you asking?"

I rolled down the window to get some air and said, "What if they start asking you all kinds of questions, what are you going to say?"

Mike just looked at me with mad confidence and said, "Toi chill, I got this under control". We pulled into the parking lot and Mike walked in like he owned the place. I sat there staring at the clock, watching the time just pass by, and an hour later Mike emerged from around the corner.

I saw Mike, but no PJ. My heart started beating so fast, I pulled the car door open and jumped out, "Where is PJ?" Mike grabbed my arm and led me back to the car. The look on his face had me so nervous I didn't know what to think. Mike looked at me with the most concerned look I had ever seen and said," Toi, you and your boyfriend owe me big time."

Mike shook his head and said," Girl, you might want to think about leaving Mr. PJ alone, he's mixed up in a lot of shit your naive ass ain't even ready for."

At this point I could have cared less about what Mike was talking about. I rolled my eyes and said, "Well is he getting out?" Mike started the car and turned up the heat, "He'll be out in a few."

I no longer wanted to talk to Mike, he had struck a nerve and he knew, but what scared me even more was that he was right. I sat in the car and looked out the window, snow started lightly dusting the window and my eyes became heavy. I sat there thinking about what I would say to PJ, I had missed my baby so much over these few weeks. I wondered if he would be proud of his little trooper. I smiled thinking about how I held my baby down.

My daydream was cut short when PJ opened the door. The wind tickled my chin as he slid across the cold leather seats. PJ wrapped his arms around me and all of my fears dissolved. I could see Mike looking through the mirror and shaking his head.

PJ kissed me on the head and leaned over, tapped Mike on his shoulder, "You know I got you man, whatever you need, I got you."

Mike looked back at him and said, "You right about that, and I intend on collecting ".

Our ride back to Boston was real quiet. I sat in the back with PJ and held him in my arms while he slept. Mike continued looking through the mirror; he didn't say a word, he just shook his head and kept on driving.

When we got back home, Mike's voice kept ringing in my ear, "You better be careful Toi." I heard his words, but they carried no fear, PJ wouldn't let anything happen to me, he had my back just like I had his.

~~~~

Time flew by when we returned from NY; me and PJ spent every day together. School was a distant memory and I knew when Chanelle found out she was going to kill me. PJ had me on a high I didn't want to come down from, but who knew I was about to have an intervention.

The weeks and days have gone by without a glitch; never in a million years would I have thought my baby could make me this happy. My soul and body were on cloud nine and it was all because of PJ. I sat on the side of the bed and thought about all the events that had taken place over the last couple of months. It is amazing to me how my life has changed since the day I laid my eyes on PJ. I have given this man my body and soul and in return he has provided me with the love I have never felt.

My face began to hurt as I smiled and thought about my man, but the phone interrupted my trance. I stood up feeling frustrated because of this phone ringing non-stop. I really wished Mike would get his own line. I picked up the phone with serious attitude, "Hello, hello!" I yell with no response coming from the other end. I look across the room at the clock and realize it's 2am, this is one of Chanelle's super late nights and I expect her home anytime now.

A ringing phone late at night always makes me nervous; my mind starts racing and I think, *God I hope my momma is ok*. I hang the phone up and return back to my bed, but ten minutes later the phone begins to ring again. I roll off the bed and think, *Damn I was almost sleeping.*

I picked up the phone and said, "WHAT!" I stood with the phone to my ear and was about to hang up when I started hearing moaning and laughing in the background. This immediately caught my attention, so I slid down on the floor and began to listen. I recognized PJ's voice and my heart dropped as I sat there listening.

I could not believe what I was hearing. PJ, on my phone, moaning and telling someone to, "Suck it harder."

I pressed my ear to the phone as hard as I could, because, I knew I did not hear what I thought I did. I sat there in disbelief for a minute and then began to scream as loud as I could "PJaaaaaayyyyyy!!!!"

After a few minutes of torture he finally hears me and says, "Oh shit," and then the phone hangs up. I sat on the floor in shock; this had to be a nightmare because I know PJ would not do this to me. I stared at the wall and tried to catch my breath. *Toi calm down*, I hear a voice in my head saying, *Toi calm down*. I put my head between my legs and begin to rock back and forth.

I finally came back around at 7 o'clock. I placed my hands on my face to see if I could feel anything. I looked across the room and saw the phone lying in the corner. I gathered enough strength to crawl across the room and grab it. I placed the phone to my chest and began to cry. God what did I do to deserve this!?

~~~~~

The thought of going to school made me ill, but Chanelle seeing me like this motivated me to get up. I managed to make it through the whole day without falling apart. I walked down the hall like the living dead and made my way to the bus. Just as I turned the corner I looked across the street out of habit and my heart dropped when I saw PJ standing there.

I stopped and stared at him because my body could not move; he walked across the street straight towards me. My face felt numb as he stood two inches away. He softly grabbed my arm and said come on. I wanted to pull away so bad, but my arm would not move.

I sat in the car and just stared out the window. I wanted to scream and punch him in the face, but I did not want to have another incident like last time.

PJ turned the music on and Keith Sweat blared through the speakers. My heart pumped to each beat, but I refused to show any emotion. PJ grabbed my hand and said, "What's up baby, you not talking to me today?"

I turned around and looked in his eyes and said, "Why PJ? I stood beside you when you went to jail. I jeopardized mine and my brother's life to help you and you treat me like this!? I have done nothing but love you from day one and you disrespect me-- tell me why?" I could no longer put on the brave face, my heart was broken and I needed him to know it. "Just tell me why, and please don't lie to me."

He just looked at me and said," I don't know why Toi, I'm sorry babe."

The blood started to rush to my brain; I looked at him with hate in my eyes and said, "Sorry, what the hell do you mean you're sorry!? I gave you my body. I trusted you and all you can say to me is you're sorry.

PJ looked at me with a blank stare and said "Toi, shut the hell up. I told you I was sorry, what the fuck you want me to do?"

I could not believe this was the man I gave my heart to-- my body was weak and my soul was lost. I tried to speak, but nothing would come out. I finally got enough strength to say, "Let me out." I was so mad and frustrated I started screaming, "PULL THE FUCK OVER…NOW! Go fuck with that nasty hoe you were dealing with last night."

We came to a light and I jumped out of the car. PJ looked at me and said, "I'm not playing with you Toi, get in the car!"

Walking was all I could do. I refused to hear any more of his rants.

Cursed by the Candy

PJ looked at me and said, "Well if this is how you want it, walk your ass home then."

I turned around and he drove off leaving me standing in the middle of the street. I felt a chill come over my body and I noticed people standing around pretending not to watch. At this point they could stare all they wanted, I could care less. The voice in my head kicked in, I placed my hands over my ears and closed my eyes tight; I just wanted to lay in the street and let it be all over. I stood there for a minute until I heard a horn blowing. I got myself together and said aloud, "Toi snap out of it!"

Finally I gathered up some strength and lifted up my head. The thought of how I was going to get home kicked in .I knew

I couldn't call Mike or Chanelle, so I did what any normal person would do in this situation, I caught the damn bus. Shit, that's what they run for.

~~~~~

Six stops later, I finally made it home and then reality kicked in with a vengeance. I couldn't believe this was happening. PJ fucked someone else last night and left me in the middle of the street; never in my lifetime would I have thought I would be going through this.

Thoughts of the last six months flooded through my brain. I realized it was all some kind of fantasy. All the time I was thinking PJ was sprung, I was playing right into his little game. His game called, "Candy Land." I was just a piece in the life of a hustler, a young naive girl with fresh jewels who would have given up her soul for a piece of the candy. I sat there in my dark room thinking, *What the hell is wrong with you Toi?* I have allowed this man to take my spirit and break down my self-esteem. I couldn't believe I was breaking my number one rule: Love thyself always. But words are easier said then done. I tried my hardest to be strong, but the pain was too intense for me to put on an act.

That little sermon I had with myself lasted for about ten minutes, my mind was wandering and the devil was knocking at my door. The thought of calling him had entered my mind a time or two, but I could not allow myself to be disrespected anymore. "Lord please take the pain away from my heart," I pleaded as I cried my self to sleep.

~~~~~

Two weeks have passed and I still have not heard from PJ. It still bothers me that he was able to let go so easy, but in reality he was never holding on. As the days pass by the pain is no longer as intense. I really think everything happens for a reason and over the last six months I had become someone I didn't even know. Chanelle and I have also become closer the last week or so; I know she has a feeling something is wrong, but she'll never say anything. That's what I love about her, she always minds her business, but in reality, if she was around a little more I would have never come across the wrath of PJ.

School is not the same since me and PJ broke up. I'm not flossing any more; it's just boring as hell. The only difference is the little boys trying to push up on me. Please... I'm hardly interested; these young boys can hardly do anything for me. They would have to borrow some money from their moms just to take me to Burger King. One thing about being with PJ is the next man better come correct or not come at all...

I can't wait for this day to be over so I can get out of this building. I walk outside and notice it is hotter then normal today. I run my hands across a jean tennis skirt I'm rocking with my crisp white sneakers. Just as I get ready to get on the bus I see PJ. I swear he looks like a Mr. Goodbar. I think to myself sooner or later I knew he would be missing me. As I was about to approach his car, I see Tonya jump in the front seat. She looks in my direction and smirks at me like, *Now what.*

I see PJ turn up his radio and kiss her on the cheek. I stood there in disbelief and asked the Lord to please give me some magical strength right now. I took a couple of deep breaths and then something happened in me and all of sudden I was calm.

The image of both of them kind of made me laugh. I turned around, pushed my hair behind my ear and said, "Enjoy my leftovers, bitch."

One thing I love about me is that I am always going to have the last word. I put my sun glasses on, turned around and got on the bus. I sat down and thought, *Demoted to Chickenhead-- never me!*

I found out from the grapevine that two weeks after that little run-in with PJ and Tonya, someone ran up on them and shot PJ's car up .I know God was the reason that I was taken out of that situation. PJ's new friend Tonya was struck by the bullet meant for PJ and died instantly. My heart ached for Tonya's family; me and Tonya were hardly friends, but I would never wish that on anyone.

I thought, PJ was lucky this time, he was only shot in the arm. God was on his side, but who knows for how long? There's always a price for living in "Candy Land".

Chanelle has been getting really restless lately. Talking about how she hates Boston and is ready to move to Virginia. I guess Sharice knew what she was talking about after all. Truth be told I am ready to get out of here also, after all the drama with PJ, this is the last place I want to be.

~~~~

Chanelle's mind is made up quickly and within a couple of months we're about to roll out. I've lived here all my life and thought of moving as scary, but then I sat back and thought about everything that has happened that made staying here seem scarier.

The day we moved everything seemed to be running smoothly, the U-Haul truck was parked outside and we were about to roll out. Mike and I were arguing about who was gong to get the last box when I looked across the street and saw PJ.

I couldn't believe he had the nerve to show up here and how did he even know I was moving? I dropped the box on the ground and walked towards him. Each step I took seemed like an eternity. I finally reached him and he reached for my hand, I pulled away from his grip and he let out a sigh.

We stood there looking in each other's eyes without speaking a word. Finally, PJ broke the silence; he said he appreciated how I had stood by him like no other and how I deserved so much more than what he gave me. I turned my head so he couldn't see the hurt I still carried around. I felt his hand on the small of my back and heard his words in my ear," Toi, I'm sorry I hurt you."

The words I heard when I noticed Mike staring at us. Mike never knew what happened between me and PJ, he just thought I took his advice and dumped him. PJ broke him off with a grand when we got back, so he was straight. I just didn't want to hear him say I told you so. This was definitely a lesson learned.

We stood at the end of the driveway with everyone's eyes glaring down our backs. PJ reached in his pocket and pulled out a diamond studded tennis bracelet he had made. He looked at me with sincerity and said, "Toi please take this so you won't forget what we had."

I looked at PJ and thought, *I will never forget him, how could I?* He was the first man to break my heart, and my first true hustler.

I pushed away from his hold and thanked him, but in the back of my mind I was thinking, *Fuck you, PJ.* He placed the bracelet on my arm and I gave him a hug. I turned around and said under my breath, **"VA here we come."**

Chapter Three

Whoever came up with Virginia is for Lovers, must have been tripping. From what I can see, Virginia is for brothers-- and fine ass ones at that.

Cultural shock is definitely what I was experiencing. Where we lived was sorta like the suburbs. There were black people around, but not like this. I felt like a kid in a candy factory, but after the drama with PJ, chilling is all I wanted to do.

Chanelle seems to be on cloud nine since she found a place for her shop. I died laughing when she told me she's calling it, "For Diva's Only". Mom is a trip.

Cursed by the Candy

School crossed my mind and I began to get nervous; I'm really not looking forward to going to school, it seems like the whole style here is different and kinda country if you ask me. I'm just going to be me and try and adapt to this place one way or another. They'll either love me or hate me.

The first day of school, I was crazy scared. Music is the only thing that seemed to calm my nerves. On the radio they were playing "It Takes Two" by Rob Base. Instantly, I got pumped up.

What to wear, what to wear? I threw on my flyest gear. A Calvin Klein jean outfit, one of my slamming pair of shoes all courtesy of PJ. I debated on whether or not to wear my bracelet. Finally I decide to rock it, show these country bumpkins what's up.

The whole idea of riding the bus sucked. I decided that day I must get my driver license. When I got off the bus the first thing I saw was a group of girls looking at me. Now this school is nothing like my old school, it's dark, grungy and smells funny.

I plaster on a fake smile and walk past the group. Of course they want to push their luck and start fucking with me. Why today Lord? You know I don't know when to keep my mouth shut .One girl says, "She thinks she's cute." It took everything for me not to turn around.

Cursed by the Candy

See one good thing about this new school situation is I have family that goes here. Sharice is going to welcome me with open arms, no doubt.

It sucks to come to a new school when your in the twelfth grade, cliques have already been established, friendships already formed. I'm like an outcast .Lucky for me, my cousin has mad flava.

I told you it's all about the genes. Cuz is also in the 12th grade. Sharice is about 5'2" and real cute. She has good hair, as we black folks like to call it. And she is also a cheerleader, so just by association I was straight .Thank goodness I saw her at the end of the hallway.

"What's up baby?" Sharice says, "Damn girl, I've been looking for you all morning."

I smiled at her and said, "Sorry I was mingling, about to get beat down on the first day of school. You know me and my mouth."

"Yeah," Sharice said with this goofy look on her face. She pulled me down the hall and said, "Let me introduce you to my friends. This is Marquetta."

I said, "What's up."

"Who do you think you are Salt and Peppa?"

I smiled at her and said, "You know it, trick". They all started laughing.

I noticed the group of females from earlier coming in our direction. They all looked at me and stopped to speak to Sharice. "Do you know her?" They asked.

Sharice said, "Yeah ,this is my family."

One of the girl's is real thick, but has this fly ass short haircut. She said, "Tell your fam to watch herself." Sharice looked at me like what the hell is going on.

Now you know I'm hardly a punk, but I thought first before this got all blown out of proportion. *My gear is too tight to get fucked up over some bullshit.* I tried to be the bigger person and make amends with the ladies, "I'm sorry if I offended you, my name is ShaToi." I reached out to shake Ms. Gorilla's hand and she dissed me and walked away. "Oh well, I tried."

From that day on, I got a lot of stares and rolling eyes. But you know my philosophy-- these bitches don't put a piece of clothing on Ms. Toi's back. So fuck 'em.

Even getting settled in I still find myself kinda down lately. Chanelle is always busy at the shop .Unfortunately that gives me lot of time to think. And an idle mind will have a sista fucked up.

The phone rings just when the depression is about to kick in, "Hello?"

"Girl what the hell is wrong with you? Sounding like someone just died."

"Sharice, shut up."

"What are you doing?" She asked.

"Nothing."

"Get your ass up and get ready, we're going out tonight."

""Where?"

Almost yelling, she says, "To a club!"

"A club, I've never been to a club. What am I going to wear?"

She started laughing and said, "All that fly shit you brought down here, you better rock it."

It was 9:30 and Sharice and Marquetta had just pulled up in my auntie's new red Volvo. I got in the car and said, "What's up ladies?"

"Nothing much," they say. "Just in search for a hustler."

Now you know that's all I needed to hear. "Candy" radar was in full effect. "Where are we going tonight? Yo' ass acting like it's all top secret and shit."

Cursed by the Candy

Sharice looked through the mirror and said, "This place called the Cotton Club." It's the spot on Thursdays. They have male strippers and everything, but after that... it's on girl. Nothing but "Ballers" up in there.

My thoughts came out loud and clear , "Shit, I feel a sweet tooth coming on."

Marquetta turned around and said, "What the hell are you talking about, are you hungry?"

I started smiling because it was time to share the love with the ladies. "Girl no, let me school you country chicks on the candy."

They both said, "What?!"

"See, the "candy" is all about the visual. A hustler with mad grip, the best clothes and a generous pocket. Must rock nothing less then a Benz, BMW or 300zx and if for some reason he is rocking a regular car, it must be kitted up. Phat rims, tint, nothing less will be acceptable. They looked at each other and said, "Damn, I know that's right. We are definitely taking her to the right place tonight."

I'm just getting to VA from up north, so I stick out like a sore thumb. Sharice pulled up to the club, and I could not believe this shit. I'm at the finest car lot on the planet .There was this brotha pulling up behind us with a hot pink Benz, then not to mention a black 325I BMW in front of us. Lawd, I was feelin' dizzy. My head was moving from left to right.

Sharice looked at me and said, "You like? "

I started moving around and said, "Girl, I'm about to cum all over myself ."

Marquetta laughed and said, "Baby girl, calm down."

We stepped out of the car. And I finally had a chance to check out my competition. I was rocking this black DKNY dress fitting to a tee. To set it off I had on some strappy black sandals .Of course a night would not be complete without jewelry.

Sharice and her girl are fly in their own VA way. But tonight all eyes were on me. My cousin is my heart, but I'm going to have to throw a little northern love her way.

We got in the club, and the excitement kicked in. First stop always the bathroom, have to make sure the makeup is on point. The moment we walked out the bathroom, Sharice was like Ms. Ghetto superstar up in here. All the dudes were like, "What's up Riccy?"

We made our way to the bar and were flocked by brotha's everywhere, "Let me get you a drink." This light dude asked me-- Now, I'm not too much into the light colored men, but this one will have to be an exception. He is rocking the most beautiful Presidential Rolex I have ever seen in my life. I thought, *This shit definitely has to be fake.* A few moments of observing this dude, I knew it was the real thing.

I'm hardly gay, but the women up in here look like models .Every piece of hair in place, makeup flawless. However, my suitor hardly seemed to be impressed, "Shorty, you want something to drink?"

"Yes, I do."

"Is Moet ok with you?" His gray eyes were hypnotizing me.

"Yeah that will be good .Will you excuse me for a minute?" I made my way over to Sharice and said, "Honey, tell me who that brotha is over their buying me some Mo?"

Sharice looked over the crowd and said, "Damn girl that's Manny. That nigga is like a millionaire."

"For real?" Was all I could say. My new friend was swamped by the madness by the time I came back.

He made room for me at the bar and said, "You've never been in here before."

I whispered in his ear, "We just moved down here from Boston."

He smirked and said, "For real. How you like it so far?"

"It's all right, but this night might change my whole perception of VA."

Manny smiled and said, "Is that right."

Now hustlers don't dance they just stand around looking cool. And Mr. Manny was doing a damn good job of it .The Moet was starting to make itself known. Manny pulled me real close and said, "Can I have your number? Maybe we can hang out sometime."

Now you know I was going to give him my number, but it wasn't going to be that easy. "What are you going to do, that would make me want to give you my number?"

Manny looked at me and said, "Baby in your wildest dreams, you have no idea what I can do for you or to you." That was it, my number was on a napkin so quick it wasn't funny.

Bitches were starting to stare, guess he was spending too much time with me. I smiled at him and said, "It looks like we have an audience."

He pulled me close and whispered, "Good."

Now an audience does nothing but motivate me more. I kissed Manny on his cheek and asked him to call me when he could.

"No doubt," he said, and I walked away.

"Sharice girl, did you see him. He was all in my face." Sharice took a sip of her drink and said, "I saw it and everyone else did to. Don't walk off by yourself any more tonight."

I looked at her like she had to be joking. "Damn it's like that?" I asked.

"Hell yeah, chicks can get mad jealous when someone new rolls up here and pulls one of the biggest hustlers in VA."

I was all fucked up and paranoid. Chicks looking at me all green eyed. I'm thinking, *Bitch please. Find some business of your own.* Just then, I looked across the club at the pool table.

There he stood, looking like a chocolate dipped cherry. Dark skinned, gold in the front of his mouth, bangin' pair of Guess jeans with a fly ass polo shirt. This nigga was rocking a herringbone chain with a medallion on it. Sharice peeped this out quick and said, "Cuz if you don't want to get killed in here tonight, don't even think about it. That's Don Don the craziest Baller in Hampton Roads."

Shit, she ain't said nothing but a thing. That just motivated me even more. Don Don, his name rolled off my tongue like butta. There was no doubt he was going to be mine. Maybe not tonight, but soon.

You know damn well, it wouldn't be a club if a fight didn't pop off. I was standing there daydreaming and my moment was interrupted from the sound of gun fire.

POP-POP!

Sharice, grabbed my arm and yelled, "Girl get down!"

"What's going on?"

"Someone is shooting, that's what's going on!"

That night we left the club and I couldn't get Don Don out of my mind. Manny had mad potential and that's an understatement .But D made my blood boil from the moment I laid eyes on him.

Friday morning rolled around and the excitement from the night before was kicking my ass. Same ole boring routine .Get up, go to school, come home. I forgot tonight there's a basketball game . Sharice will be cheering. Damn, I guess I can go with Marquetta. You know I don't trust no chicks, but what are my other options. It's better than staying in the house.

Night time rolls around and I am designer down from head to toe. Must be on point at all times. Marquetta picks me up around seven and her outfit is ok, but that's cool, I don't need her trying to out shine me anyway. Finally we get in the game a half hour later .The traffic was ridiculous. D catches my eye the moment we walk in. This has to be fate. I look around to see if I can spot Sharice.

Cursed by the Candy

I wonder if it's because I am new or they're just hating-- stares coming from all directions. Shit, you wanna stare. I'll give you something to stare at.

A piece of paper drops out of my hand. I rock the most seductive dip and pick it up. I even throw my hair behind my shoulder and step down the bleachers. Now stare at that!

Finally I spot Sharice and give her a quick hug, "Are you ok ,after last night's drama?"

"I'm straight. Girl sit over there and watch us burn this place up!"

I yell, "Go represent for the fam!"

And that she did. They were out there flipping and pumping. Now Norview's squad is tight. They were like a ghetto super squad.

Well, I guess my little dip must have been effective. I turned around and Don Don was about to sit down next to me. *Toi calm down.* My heart started pumping all hard. I swear, he'll be able to see it through my shirt .

I'm trying to play it cool, like I don't even see him. All I smell is the scent of Eternity flowing all through my body .This nigga had me in a trance.

"What's up girl, you know Riccy ?"

"Yeah ,that's my family."

He replies, "I see the resemblance."

You would have thought I actually gave a damn about this game.

"I saw you giving everybody a little show earlier." *Goodness. Was I that obvious? I'm gonna have to work on that.*

"What are you talking about?"

"Don't trip, it's all good. I liked what I saw. Those jeans you have on are on point. You must not be from around here. Bitches don't dress like that down south."

I was fully aware of this already. I reply, "I'm from Boston." What are you doing after the game he asked."

"Whatever Sharice is doing."

"Well, I guess I'll see you later. Riccy always knows what's up." D walks away, and I feel an urge to call him back.

We never did go out that night; my cuz fell and pulled a muscle in her leg. The weekend was still young though and I was hopeful that we would make it out before the end. When I made it home that night I had a message from Manny. Dag he called already…hum.

We talked and he asks me if I wanted to go to dinner with him. I said yes, and we agreed to hook up the next day.

Cursed by the Candy

Daydreaming seems to have become my hobby. I was thinking about my cousin and her friend Marquetta. After a while, I started to observe her behavior. Marquetta is a real pretty girl with mad potential, but it had to be nurtured some more. In time, with the right training, home girl could be untouchable. Now Marquetta liked hustlers, but not to my personal standards. The brotha's had dough no doubt, but they were moneymakers not straight up ballers.

Let me educate you on the course I call, "Hustler 101". See there are three levels of the ultimate player in the game: **First** you see, there's what I like to call, the money makers. Those are the street corner boys, the dope house brotha's. **Then** we have my beloved, "Ballers"; these are the people who benefit from the moneymakers. **Last** but definitely not least, we have the all almighty "Dons". These brotha's go by any means necessary to make sure their dough flows like a chocolate river .They have no problem, and don't even think twice when it comes down to the Benjies. They will eliminate anyone whether you are a moneymaker, baller or a person in the wrong place at the wrong time.

In their eyes you are replaceable. The word friend does not exist in the game. Trust no one, that's their moto. Players believe the candy must always flow, no distractions.

When these guys are initiated into this lifestyle, it's usually for keeps .Their goal is to live the hustler's dream-- The big candy in the sky. So the Don is like God.

Ms. Toi prides herself on being observant, it's a must. And from what I have observed, the ballers roll in Land Cruisers, Acuras or anything else that will make you do a double-take. They don't stand in lines and have VIP in all the tightest spots. Better believe they drink nothing less then Cristal or Moet. And occasionally Henny, you know Hen Dog? Ok, Hennessy for you slow to catch on.

Now, on the other hand, Don's are chauffeured around by their bodyguards, drink liquors you can't even pronounce. They don't sit in VIP, because they own the club. Listen up and be sure to take notes, because I'm just getting started.

See I've never been the type to hang out with a lot of chicks. The way I feel, females are nothing but trouble. The green eyed devil they are. Ms. Chanelle schooled me early, she would say, "Toi, don't trust a bitch." Momma knows what she's talking about and I have all the faith in her words of wisdom. Why wouldn't I? She works in the devil's layer every day. The hair salon is the gossiping capital for females.

Momma would say, "Toi let me tell you how these trifling heifers were in the shop today running their mouths. Talking about this person and that person .Who's man bought them a new car or who just got locked up."

I sit there listening to Chanelle thinking, *Please, bitches, get a life. Who has time for the yapping lips of the female species?*

Ms. Toi must stay focused. Now if you're going to relay some info on who just got locked up or who the next baller in place is, I am all ears. However, the other petty messes must cease.

Reality kicks back in and I start focusing on my date with Manny.

Manny picks me up and to say I'm gorgeous would be an understatement. He's mad laid back, like a lion searching for his prey. And tonight that happens to be me. It's all love though. I'm enjoying the attention.

The restaurant was beautiful. It sat on the beach and was called The Lighthouse.

The atmosphere is more then anyone my age is used to. But I'm going to act like this is the norm. Always remember to play your position.

Damn, I don't know what's wrong with me. I'm sitting here with this man that any girl would be flattered to even be acquainted with, looking at him…feeling nothing. Emotionally he doesn't have me wondering *what if*, physically my jewels are as dry as the desert, but of course all that can change once I get a taste of the candy. From dealing with men in this lifestyle you must always show respect. Even if you're not interested .They have ass thrown at them left and right. Rejection is not even a part of their vocabulary. Play it wrong, you may be found burned in a lake somewhere.

What's strange about the whole thing is, the more I try and push Manny away the more persistent he becomes. It's kinda scary. We leave the restaurant and of course the first thing that comes out of his mouth is, "What's up next, Toi? My condo is on the beach."

I'm thinking, *Shit how convenient.* What did I expect, though? He just spent 200.00 on dinner, now he wants something in return. That something just so happens to be me.

Can't deny the fact that the body is definitely aching for some loving.

Quickly I think, *Should I lay it on him hard or just give him a little taste?*

This could be beneficial. I break down and say, "Baby whatever you want to do." Hell, I don't know were I am anyway. I'm not trying to be put out on the side of the road somewhere.

Manny's spot looks like something out of "Scar Face". To say this place was laid would be an insult. We drive around a circular driveway, up to the front of the beach house. It stood high on stilts as the water flowed below.

Manny says, "Make yourself comfortable." I'm thinking, *You don't have to tell me twice.* I take my sandals off and sit on this beautiful white leather sectional. He touches my shoulders from behind and says, "Would you like to watch TV or listen to some music?" I opt for TV, that way I don't have to talk much.

He brings out two glasses of Don and asks me to lay back on the couch. I try and position myself back comfortably and Manny grabs my arms and pins me down, "What's up baby?" I was just trying not to sound scared as hell. He begins to unbutton my shirt ,but gets impatient and rips it open. My throat gets dry and I'm thinking this nigga is about to rape me. He opens my bra and starts licking my nipple like a lollipop. I instantly relax; I haven't had a man's touch since PJ. My body is definitely starving for some affection. Manny stops and looks in my eyes with the intensity of a cat. "Get up and let's go upstairs," he says.

I slowly walk up the spiral staircase wondering I have gotten myself into. Manny lays down on the bed as if he was a King. Right now, I'm hardly feeling like a Queen. He looks over at me and says, "Toi, come stand over me." Slowly, I stand over him as instructed. A seductive smile takes control of my face as I think about him indulging in my jewels.

Out of the blue he says, "Give me some of that candy rain."

I stare at him with a blank stare and respond, "Baby, I don't know what that is."

In a harsh tone Manny says, "Make that pussy flow!" My ears must be playing tricks on me. I know damn well this nigga doesn't want me to piss on him. Slowly, I lower my body on top of his. He moans and I think, *Thank goodness.* When I think I am home free he grabs me by my hair and swings me back on the bed. "Bitch, don't ever disobey me!" Manny snatches me up and pushes me against a window that stretches all across his bedroom.

All I can see is the moonlight shining on the ocean. I gasp for air as he penetrates me with such force. I hear my voice come through as a whisper, "Momma help." Then the tears escape my eyes.

Manny removes his body from mine and speaks somehow in a harsh but mellow tone all at once, "Get your shit and get the fuck out."

He walks over to the bed and throws my clothes at me as if I were a dog. I sat on the floor feeling like a scolded child. My eyes were shut tight and something took over my feeling of defeat. A rush of heat absorbed my body and I yelled, "What the hell is wrong with you!?"

Before I could get another word out of my mouth, I saw a flicker of light. And I fell across the dresser.

Manny picks me up as I struggle to get my balance. He opens the door and pushes me. The side railing stops my fall. "Get your dumb ass home the best way you can." The door slams shut. I feel the cold ocean air surround my body.

Just then, I hear Channel's voice as clear as day, "Get your ass up right now, the reason this man treated you this way is because you let yourself slip. Do what you need to do and get your black ass home!" I looked up at the moon and gathered my strength. Stood up and wiped my face with my hands.

Ok, Toi men are like dogs. Throw his ass a bone and get out of here.

As I walk over to the door, my heart starts thumping so hard I swear it's about to come through my skin. Manny finally decides to open the door. "What the fuck do you want?"

Sincerity was all over my face when I said, "Baby, I am sorry I didn't do what you asked." Disbelief and anger is the way I would describe his expression.

I reached out with caution and guided him towards the door. Slowly I dropped to my knees and handled Mr. Manny like he was a tootsie roll pop. I was searching for how many licks it took to get to the center and that for me would be home.

Manny, finally became satisfied with my performance and gently grabbed my chin. He guided me towards his face and said, "Toi if you want to play with the big dogs treat them like kings and you'll be rewarded. Treat a nigga with disrespect, what I did to you tonight will seem like a game."

Cursed by the Candy

Every word he said, I already knew. I just slipped for a minute and forgot one of my rules. Of course by now you should know it's always-- Play your position.

Manny took me home that night and acted like nothing had ever happened. But in his world this was nothing. However, for Ms. Toi a valuable lesson was learned. If you want to play with the big boys, you must be prepared mentally and physically. And from tonight's encounter, I've realized, I'm not.

Yeah, Manny is a bit out of my league. I have no desire to be in Norfolk General in a coma or in prison with Manny. As of tonight, Ms. Toi throws in the white towel. Super size Hershey bars are too much for me. I'll just stick with the Hershey kisses.

Chapter 4

I never said anything to Sharice about the drama with Manny. Everybody doesn't need to be in my business. You know, females are weird creatures. Yes, Sharice is my cousin, but chicks are chicks. And I don't trust 'em.

Don't get me wrong she's mad cool. And very smart, I mean book smart .Pretty and smart, that is a deadly combination if you know how to work it right. Sharice will hang out with the players, but she doesn't allow them in her "real world ". She'll tell you in a minute that everything that glitters isn't gold. She's staying focused on college, Spellman in fact. I really admire her for that. Not all into the other man's candy, but in search of her own.

Thinking about Sharice so much I decided to give her a call." What's up girl, what are you doing?"

"Studying, something you know nothing about."

"Whatever girl, you want to go to the mall, Chanelle left me some money .I'll buy you something."

Sharice says, "Damn right. What do you mean you'll buy me something. Something or an outfit?"

Cursed by the Candy

"Bitch damn .I should have caught a cab it would have been cheaper .What time are you going to be here?"

"In about an hour," she said.

All of a sudden I feel this strange sensation on my vagina. Quickly, I take my panties down to inspect. This weird looking spider thing is crawling on my pubic hairs." I know this nigga didn't give me crabs!" Immediately I grab the clippers and start shaving the hair off. This is so nasty.

You would have thought my life was over the way I was scrubbing. By the time Sharice arrived I was all messed up.

"Girl, can you take me to the drug store?"

Sharice says, "Yeah, what do you need to get?"

I want to tell her so bad, but I can't. "My period started I need some tampons."

When we get to the mall Sharice looks at me and says, "Damn girl, you're too quiet for me. What's wrong?"

A lump swells up in my throat and I turn to face the window. I gather myself together and say," Come on girl, let's go and spend some of Chanelle's money."

Instantly I was cured when I stepped into the mall. Damn this is the place to be .This mall was nothing but the truth. "Candy" everywhere; we looked in a couple of stores, but I was definitely not focused. There were men everywhere.

Sharice tapped me on the shoulder and instantly knocked me out of my trance. "Would that over there brighten up your mood?" I turned around and my eye's locked right on him .A headache was about to come on from me staring so hard.

It was Don Don over there surrounded by an entourage of females and dudes .You would have thought he was the Prez or something, and they were his secret service agents.

Sharice knew exactly what was up." You think you can handle that? I told you home boy has some issues." Her voice became a blur. My focus was on D.

"Let's go over to the food court," I say, almost pulling her arm off.

"Damn girl calm down."

As I get closer, D looks up and we make eye contact. We get in line to get a drink, and I see him coming towards us, "What's up Riccy?"

She looks at him and says, "What's up?"

"Hey you," he says and pulls on my shirt. You and your fam didn't make it out the other night.

Cursed by the Candy

I responded," No, Ms. Riccy had to be super cheerleader and pull a muscle. We all laughed .Thinking to myself, *I wish she'd go over there somewhere.* Sharice must have felt my vibe, because she says I'll be right back Toi.

She walks away and leaves me alone with D. I'm standing their feeling all stupid like I don't know what to say. And that's totally out of character for me.

"Girl, snap out of it, this is the moment you have been waiting for."

To me he's the only person in this mall, I want him to feel the energy I'm feeling .I start speaking to him soft but sternly, "So what's up? Your all up in here with your posse .He says, "Nah, that's just some people I know."

"Oh, I see." D moves close to me and I smell that Polo cologne loud and clear .Damn this nigga smells good, I'm about to melt right here on the floor.

He was standing so close to me now, I could smell the Tic Tacs on his breath. I wished I was one of them.

"So what's good for tonight?" D says. Me and some of my boys are rolling out to David's tonight, you wanna come?"

"I'll ask Sharice when she comes back."

"Oh yeah, I forgot you have to be 21 to get in, but I know some people so you'll be straight."

Nigga please, I say to my self.

"Look, Ms. Toi is always prepared sweetie, don't worry about that." I pulled out my wallet and found my fake ID's, "In fact I have two. One that says I am 22 and another that says 25, for those old head clubs."

"See, I am officially 22 .There will be no problem and Sharice has one too.

D says, "Oh shit let me find out you have the hook up."

"D, you forgot I am from up North, you can get anything you want if you have some dough-- fake ID's, social security numbers, birth certificates. Name it, you can buy it with the correct amount.

D looked like I had just insulted him "Shorty don't get it twisted, money is never an issue with me, remember that."

Just then Riccy walks up. *Thank goodness*, I say to myself, things were starting to get a little tense up in here. "Hey girl, D just invited us to David's tonight, you wanna go?"

Sharice yells like she just won the lottery or something, "Hell yeah, I wanna go girl!"

Cursed by the Candy

"Well it looks official like we'll be going tonight."

D says, "Cool," and pulls out a wad of money. He hands it to me and says, "Go buy yourself something nice for tonight. He asks for a hug and gives me his beeper number.

I look at Sharice and grab her, "Oh my God girl, he just gave me $600 dollars."

Riccy looks at me and says, "Everything that glitters isn't gold, remember that. Cuz, you know I love you. Don't get caught up with the "candy" as you call it .Go get you something nice, just get me a pair of shoes. I'll spend Auntie Chanelle's money."

She whispers under her breath, "That money was earned, it means more."

"Whatever. Let's go spend the easy money *and* the hard earned money; it's all the same to me."

Everything else was pretty uneventful after that. My cuz was working on my nerves. Enough female bonding for me today. Her little comment had me pissed off, but she had no problem finding a $200 dollar pair of shoes.

Never mind the creatures still crawling between my legs, ugh, damn!

"Riccy, you ready to go? I'm starting to have cramps and I want to rest before tonight."

Cursed by the Candy

"Yeah girl let's go."

As soon as I reached the front door the sweet aroma of Chanelle throwing down was all in the air. See my momma not only can do some hair, but she can throw down in the kitchen. We need to open up a restaurant. Moms has mad skills, she is sorta a renaissance women .Talented in many areas.

I approach the kitchen and I am thrown by a unfamiliar voice of a man.

"Hey momma, how ya doing? I thought I was going to have to put out a missing persons report on you. "Very funny, you a comedian now? I hugged Chanelle and realized just how much I'd missed her.

See Toi, momma still knows how to cook .I smile and say, "Oh you got jokes now." We all start laughing, then I turn around and say, "and may I ask who this gentlemen is you're cooking for?"

"Oh, I'm sorry, excuse my rudeness. Charles, this is Toi my daughter .I approach him like a daddy sizing up his daughter's first date .He extends his hand to mine and says, "Nice to finally get a chance to meet you. I've heard so many things about you and your brother."

Oh really, because I've never heard anything about you. Chanelle turns around and gives me that momma look, like you better shut up now. I shake home boy's hand and indulged in some small talk for a minute. Guess he seems ok, but I'm not too sure. He was staring way too much for my liking.

I went upstairs to get mentally and physically prepared for tonight .Remember, impressions are always important. Toi must make a good one at all times, especially tonight .See, I'm not only trying to turn D's head ,but any other ballers that might have tight grip too. There's no mistaking that D is my number one priority for the night, but Toi must always keep her options open.

There are no words to explain the outfit I am wearing tonight. The only one that comes to mind is-- fabulous. Chanelle pulled herself away from Charles long enough to hook up my hair, and damn did she do her thing. I looked at my watch and started to get impatient waiting on Riccy.

A drink would set this night right off. I pull some private stock out of my stash .I think to myself, *D doesn't know what he's in for tonight. For that matter.... do I?"*

I beeped him and let him know we were on our way. Fifteen minutes later he called me back, "Yo someone call D?"

"Yeah, I called you, it's Toi."

"What's up girl, you coming out? "

"Yeah, as soon as my slow cousin gets here."

"Alright shorty, I'll be looking for you. Although it won't be hard to spot you."

"Whatever, I'll see you later." I hang up the phone with a big Kool-Aid smile plastered on my face. I'm starting to feel nervous, and my mind is moving fast and furious. I start thinking about all of the drama I went through with PJ and Manny and hope this is some how different.

I ask God to please let this experience be better. My inner voice comes through loud and brings me back to reality, *How dare you ask the Lord to help you with the devil's work?!* I start to cry and the tears just stream down my face, *Hush please, not now.*

Chanelle's voice interrupts my thoughts, "Baby, Sharice is down here." I went in the bathroom and fixed up my face. Took a deep breath and said, "Toi put that smile back on, and have a good time."

When I got downstairs my mouth dropped open when I saw Sharice, "Dang girl, you almost look as good as me."

Sharice spins around and says, "No I look better then you tonight trick. Chanelle clears her throat and starts getting all happy. "

"Look at my little Diva's in training. Watch out VA, here comes Toi and Riccy."

I look at my moms like, please. "Sharice you ready?"

"Yeah girl let's go."

We get in the car and I ask Sharice about Marquetta, "Where has Marquetta been lately?"

"Girl she's falling all in love with this dude. He has her on house arrest."

"Damn it's like that? I hope that brotha has some dough and she's not giving that cootie cat away for free."

Sharice shakes her head and says, "I know that's right. Take me to dinner or something."

"Shit, I'll take a card… something… to at least let me know you appreciate the goodies." I snicker to myself, I knew the candy had to be flowing somewhere in her veins, it would be unnatural for it not to be.

"I talked to D earlier and he said he would be looking out for us.

"No," Sharice said, "he'll be looking for you, Toi. I've known D for a minute now and I have never seen him respond to a female like this before, especially someone he just met. I know you think you have everything under control, but D has a reputation of being all about his business and extremely demanding. Word is out that he even knocked off a couple of brotha's just for getting in his way. I listened to Sharice and took in every word; I went through everything she said with a fine tooth comb: *Ok-- D's all about business so what I'll do is mind my business and that equates to me "playing my position". Next, he is very demanding, shit so am I, I demand that you show me respect and in return I will always be available on demand to handle our business, no questions asked.*

See ladies this is how a real baller requires his female to act. And last but not least, as far knocking brotha's out, well that is to be expected in this line of work. But don't get it twisted I have no intentions in being an accomplice to anyone. The less I know the better; I need to be able to pass a polygraph test on demand. Ms. Toi doesn't need to know a damn thing.

I told you before that I am very observant and one thing that I have noticed about brotha's in the game is they will kill another man at the drop of a dime. Then they have to worry about the man's entourage coming after them. The way I see it is, if you mess them up mentally to the point they think they are about too lose their mind, you would benefit more in the long run. Player's are already paranoid as hell, so just add that to your advantage, and play on their paranoia, 'cause their game can be bent all out of whack.

Make them think their best friend is being shady, and sooner or later they will cause their own demise. Play it right like that, and you will walk away with squeaky clean hands. This is why if all the players in the game were females, everything would run so differently. See females plan everything out, we don't just jump into things. They're would be fewer murders and more dough .And definitely fewer black men in the system .There is more than enough candy for everyone to be happy. But don't take Toi's word for it, this is only my opinion.

Sharice looks over at me and says, "What are you over their thinking about?"

"Girl, nothing really."

We finally get to David's and practically get in a fight over a damn parking space. We step out the car and I feel like I am about to walk down the red carpet at an awards show or something .I am not exaggerating when I say all eyes were on us . When we enter the club I see D immediately; he approaches us and says, "What's up ladies, let's go upstairs to the VIP area."

I turn around and look for Riccy and she is talking to some chicks, "Riccy let's go upstairs", and do you know these heifers had the nerve to look at me like I was crazy. Sharice noticed the ghetto about to come out of me, so she wrapped her conversation and joined us.

"Damn, Sharice what's up with your friends?"

She grabs my arm and says, "Don't get all ghetto fabulous on me now."

The VIP section was laid out, and everybody in there looked like they belonged. Just like at the last club, females everywhere looking like they just stepped out of a magazine. D grabs my hand and leads me over to the couch .

Now home boy looked real nice tonight, but something about him was a bit off .Once we sat down I whispered in his ear ,"How are you doing tonight? You look a little tired."

He smiled and squeezed my hand. "I'm cool baby, but this headache is kicking my ass. "You and Sharice want something to drink? "

"Yeah, that would be good." D calls the waitress over and orders a bottle of Moet and a glass of Hennessy .Were sitting their talking enjoying ourselves when guess who walks in with two chicks-- Manny. He walks directly towards us with the females on his heels.

He reaches us and gives D a pound, they exchange a few words and he walks away. Just as he is about to turn away, he stops and says, "Hey, Toi you looking good tonight."

"Thank you", I reply feeling like I want to spit in his nasty face. He smiles and walks away. This playing your position is starting to wear me down.

D looks over at me and says, "I didn't know you knew Manny."

"Yeah, I met him the last time me and Sharice went out. Sharice what's the name of that club you took me to?"

"Mr. Magic's," she replies. Just as Riccy gets the last word out of her mouth, this light bright girl approaches us. She walks right in between me and D, as if I were not even sitting there.

"D, what time are you leaving?"

He looks at her, and if looks could kill she would have been dead, "Tammy, don't you see I'm busy right now? "

She looks over at me and says, "I don't give a damn about this bitch sitting here." Sharice looks at me like, "Oh shit," but I refuse to play into this heifer's little fit. "D, excuse us for a moment were going to the restroom." I lean over, look her dead in the eye and kiss him on the cheek. I stand up and pull my skirt down and walk away twisting my ass slow and smooth .Sharice couldn't wait for us to get in the bathroom.

"Girl I knew you were about to go off!"

"You know it took everything in me not to smack the shit out of her. Girl, my hands were starting to sweat and I was getting mad as hell, but D's not my man, so he needs to handle his business."

We went back upstairs to find D playing pool with Manny, the chick was nowhere to be found .Sharice saw some dudes she knew so I followed her over to talk to them .I didn't want it to look like I was being disrespectful so I walked back over to D.

He saw me coming and said, "Yo man, that's it for me. Manny looked over at me and winked, and kept his game going on.

"I see you got rid of Ms. Fatal Attraction."

"Oh your real funny."

"You need to have your women in check better than that."

He smiles at me and says,"I do, that's why you handled yourself like a lady, thank you." Keith Sweat's, "Make it last forever" came on, and I asked D if he wanted to dance.

"Nah, shorty, how about we get out of here, my head is really bothering me now."

I found Sharice with those girls that were grilling me earlier."Cuz you mind if I leave with D?"

Riccy replied, "Naw girl go handle your business."

I feel fire on my back from all the haters who were staring with that green glare coming from their eyes-- jealously. D scopes it out immediately, and says, "Come on Toi." He puts his hand on the small of my back and guides me towards the door.

The valet pulls up in D's cream-colored Jaguar. "D, I can drive if you're feeling too bad."

"Thanks, but I'm all right." I place my hand on the back of his neck and start massaging it gently. "That feels good girl." I just smile and close my eyes and listen to slow jams playing on the radio. "You want something to eat," he asks.

"Yeah, I am a little hungry."

"Ok, Waffelhouse or IHOP?"

"How about your house, I can fix you something to eat and you can lie down."

He starts laughing and says, "Girl do you really know how to cook or are you going to kill me?"

"Please a sista can cook, you'll see."

We pull up to D's spot and I notice it was not as extravagant as Manny's, but it was still real nice. He lived in a two-bedroom condo in Virginia Beach, a nice community with a playground and everything. I get out of the car and I notice D reaching for something under his seat. He pulls a gun out and places it in his waistband. When we get to the front door he pushes in a combination on the screen door .Then he pulls out a remote to unlock the top lock and a key for the bottom. Damn this place is like Fort Knox, but hell if anyone was ever after him he would be dead before he could get in the house.

The inside of the house was laid out; everything was black and burgundy lacquer. Classy, but I had expected that from him.

"So, what do you have to eat in here?"

"Go look in the kitchen. I'm going to take some Tylenol. I went in the fridge and I was amazed at all the food he had. I decided to make some waffles, bacon and eggs .It seemed like D was gone forever. I had finished cooking and everything when I finally called out to him, "D, are you ok?"

No answer so I tried again .This time he answered, "Yeah Toi, I'm on the phone, I'll be out in a minute . A few minutes later he was coming down the hall, "Damn girl it smells good in here; you even set the table. What are you trying to do, spoil a brotha?"

I gave him this silly look and said, "If that's what you want." We had a nice meal, and curled up on the couch. I looked down and D was fast asleep in my lap .I just sat their watching him sleep, imagining if this was my house and he was my man. Maybe one day, but for now I'll just take it day by day.

I woke D up about an hour later ,my leg and my neck felt like they were about to break. "Baby can we go lie down in your bed?"

He sat up and said, "Yeah." I sat on the bed and grabbed a pillow. He followed me and said, "Put this on and lay down on your back. The tee shirt fit like it was made just for me.

D crawled in between my legs and laid his head on my stomach. I was in total disbelief.

He had my heart the first night .Our connection was powerful. Sex wasn't involved; the bond was formed from a simple touch. As I watched him sleeping, I wondered if he only let his guard down because he felt bad. The next morning he was up early and back to his usual self.

The night we had shared seemed like a dream. He was so distant, like we hadn't spent the night in each other's arms.

"What are you doing today?" D asked.

"Nothing, probably helping Chanelle at the shop .Why, what are you doing?"

D started smiling and said "Shorty making money. I looked at him and said, "I heard that." I must admit I was disappointed.

"You ready to go Toi ? I need to get outta here."

"Yeah, whenever you are." D took me home and we sat in the driveway for a minute talking.

"I had a good time last night. "

"Oh really you use to niggas's falling asleep on you? If that's the case I can't mess with you. I need to be entertained at all times. Don't make this a habit."

I sat their thinking, *This nigga must have me mixed up with one of these whack VA chicks. Who does he think I am?* See, Im about two seconds from going postal on this brotha.

D grabs my hand and says, "Chill, girl I was only fucking with you. Can you get out tonight? I promise there will be no sleeping." I leaned forward and kissed him on his cheek. You know a sista's breath was still kicking.

As soon as I walked in the house I was greeted by mouth almighty, "Damn ,how long we been down here, three months and Ms. Toi already found a "Candy Man". That's my sista, gold digger number one."

I reply, "Shut up, you just mad these hoochies around here not paying your ass no attention .Were is Chanelle?"

"With her man Charles. They just left and your grown ass is in trouble."

"For what?"

Mike starts laughing and says, "I forgot when your ass became grown and started staying out all night. And you're real bold, had the nerve to have the brotha drop you off in the driveway."

"Whatever, mind your business!"

I went up stairs and called momma, "Hello, for Diva's Only ".

I paused and said, "Hey momma."

"Hey, where the hell have you been?"

"I stayed over Riccy's last night."

"Stop lying Toi. We'll talk about this later. I need you to get down here and wash some hair. Have Mike bring you." She slams the phone down and my stomach dropped to my knees. Chanelle was really pissed. I sat down on my bed and thought, *Lawd this is going to be a long day.*

Believe it or not, Chanelle really didn't bother me at all. I guess her mind was all on Mr. Charles. Every time I looked around he was right there, under her ass. Now, I know I sound like a spoiled brat, but I'm happy for Chanelle. At least he's keeping her out of my hair. But his wandering eyes still give me the creeps. I noticed it again today, now I know it's not my imagination.

I passed the hell out that evening. Chanelle didn't nag me, but she sure worked the hell out of me. I finally woke up around 9:30. I sure hope Chanelle stays over at home boy's house tonight.

My growling stomach interrupts my thoughts. I go downstairs and hear all this moaning. I look in the den and see Mike's ass sitting on the couch with this nasty hoe. Immediately I recognize her. This is one of the females that hates on me at school all the time. It was wrong, but I couldn't help myself.

"Excuse me, can you two keep it down? " Yeah, I wanted her ass to see my face. I grabbed my sandwich and went back to my room.

As soon as I reached for the phone to call D, it rang, "Hello."

"Toi what are you doing?"

"Nothing ma, why?" I'm staying over at Charles's house tonight. Call me if you need something."

As she was about to hang up I said, "Can we go shopping tomorrow?"

Toi, I didn't forget about you lying to me. "But ma."

"Toi don't even try it. I know one thing, you better not bring no babies up in my house."

"I'm not ma, goodnight. "

Finally, I paged D and an hour later and he called back. "What's up shorty?"

"I don't know, you tell me," there was a lot of noise in the background, when he said," I'm still handling business, but be ready in about an hour."

I took another bath and waited for D to pick me up. Just like he said, an hour later he was outside. Damn, his chocolate ass looked good that night. You know, sexy in a rugged kind of way. I couldn't help but to lean over and give him a real kiss. His lips tasted like chocolate syrup. I could have sucked them all night.

He pulled away and said, "Damn, girl it's like that?"

I said, "It's anyway you want it, D".

D and I went to have breakfast as planned. I couldn't wait to get out of there. I only had one thing on my mind. Every time I thought about what I was going to do to him tonight, I could feel the sweetness dripping down my leg.

"Toi, I need to make a run real quick .That cool "? D turns the radio on and they're playing a cut by EPMD. He starts flowing to it, and getting a bit excited. I look over at the speedometer and it says 95 mph. My heart starts beating real fast. He must have noticed I was getting scared, because he slowed down. He started smiling and said, "I got this." For some reason his words put me totally at ease. I grabbed his hand, closed my eyes and flowed to the music with him.

Cursed by the Candy

We pulled up into these apartments and D grabbed something from under the seat. "I'll be right back."

About twenty minutes had passed and I noticed this girl and guy fighting in the parking lot. I tried my hardest not to be nosey, but I couldn't help it. The guy screamed, "YOU DUMB BITCH!" And then he pushed her on the ground. She tried to get up, but he kicked her. I was staring real hard when I noticed it was Marquetta. *Oh my goodness.* I looked around to see if anyone else was watching. I was about to jump out the car when D came back.

"What are you doing? You better mind your business, that's how shit pops off."

"D that's my girl, I can't just leave."

"Yes the hell you can, she doesn't even know you're over here. Toi, you must remember, dealing with me, you gonna have to turn your head to a lot of things. That's the only way I can have it! What you gonna do? Call the police. Then all our asses be in jail. I'm sorry baby, we gotta go."

He pulled off and I felt a knot form in my stomach. The ride to D's house was kinda quiet after that. I felt so bad. *What if he kills her or something?* I knew I couldn't allow my mind to get the best of me. D was right, I need to mind my business.

I glanced over at my baby and admired his strong features; he was looking like a king tonight. He was so laid back, and sure of himself. That alone was a turn on. When we're together everything seems to just flow. Games are not required. I can just be myself.

I reach over for D's hand and he places mine in his lap. The clock was now reading 1:30 a.m. I was tired as hell, but tonight was not to be about sleeping .Other things were on my mind. The slow jams that were playing, had mellowed us both out. I took full advantage of this opportunity.

Slowly, I started rubbing my hands on D's groin. He looks over and smirks, "It's all good." That's all I needed to enhance my game of seduction.

I unzipped his pants and put my finger in his mouth to get it wet. I massaged his manhood slow and then picked up the pace. D started to squirm and moan a bit. He pulled the back of my hair and said, "Toi, stop before you make me crash, for real."

I started laughing and said, "What's wrong, you can't handle it?"

He allowed me to entertain him awhile before he said, "Talk shit now, wait till later." A smile gained control of my face. I kissed him on the cheek, and glared out of the sunroof .This was a picture perfect night, the stars were so bright it looked like a painting. My daydream was cut short when his pager went off.

D looked down and said, "911, I need to make this call ". He pulled over to the side of the road and stepped out. I tried to read the expression on his face. A blind man could tell something was terribly wrong. He hit the side of the car and scared the shit out of me.

I got out and asked, "What's wrong?"

D just stared into the blue and said,"Toi, get back in the car. I need to take you home!"

D was driving like a bat outta hell. I had to know what was going on. "Baby, talk to me."

He took a breath and said, "My boy Manny got shot tonight, he's dead."

I was silent, my feelings were all crazy. Shit, Manny did just beat my ass the other night. However, the human part of me kicked in. I allowed myself to feel sad for a moment. The feelings of grief really only appeared because D was bothered. And I was grieving for him.

"I'm sorry about your friend, baby." Shit, I figure whatever happened between me and Manny died right along with him.

D turned up the music, no more slow jams. It was strictly Naughty by Nature. D's state of mind had been replaced with business. He escaped into his own world after that and I understood.

I closed my eyes and allowed myself to feel for Manny and his family. Yes, he was fucked up to me, but he was someone's son. And for that I showed respect.

D dropped me off and I couldn't wait to hit the bed.

I was awakened shortly after by a loud noise. *What in world was that?* It seemed to take me forever to reach the bottom of the steps. I looked around and saw Mike sitting in the kitchen.

"Why are you making all that noise?"

Mike looked at me with fear in his eyes. "Toi, I'm not in the mood for your shit to today."

"I'm not going to mess with you, boy. What's wrong?"

"That nasty bitch burned me."

I sat their wondering for a moment who he was talking about. Mike has so much company, I had no idea which flava of the week he was speaking of.

"Well, who were you talking to on the phone?" Mike obviously was annoyed.

"Momma, nothing like this has ever happened to me before."

"Well, calm down it's not like you gonna die."

"How in the hell do you know! Shit, she might have AIDS or something."

"Well you weren't thinking about that when you were hitting it raw." Immediately, I wished I could take that back. Manny had just put me in this situation. I would have been livid if someone said that to me.

My brother was hurting and I was definitely not used to that. I tried to lighten up the mood. "Stop looking all crazy, butthead. Ma will take care of you." I embraced Mike and went back to bed.

~~~~~

The following morning I was awakened by Chanelle's voice. The moment I hit the last stair I saw Charles. *Damn, can she piss without him?* He is really starting to get on my nerves.

"Good morning, Ma. Did you get a chance to talk to Mike?""

"Yeah...why?"

"I was just asking. Can we go to the mall today?"

Chanelle looked up from her mail and said "What do you need?" This conversation was headed in the wrong direction and I could feel it.

"Some shoes and other stuff." I could tell that her mind was in some other place.

Finally she gave me a bit of attention and said "Baby, I'll give you the money. Me and Charles already had something planned. And I have a ton of bookkeeping to do."

My eyes became small, as I tried to fight back the tears, "Ma, can I talk to you for a minute....alone?" Chanelle looks at Charles as though she is asking for permission .The moment we left the room I no longer could contain my frustration. "Ma, we haven't spent any time together in weeks. It's all about your man, what about me? Since you've found a new bed buddy you act like you don't have any kids!"

The sting on my face was instant.

"Who in the hell do you think you are, talking to me like that?!" I tried to interrupt her, but she cut me off, "Shut up Toi and sit your spoiled ass down! I work seven days a week. Give you anything that you ask for. I listen to your problems and never say a word, even if I don't agree. You will not disrespect me. Where in the world did I go wrong for you to even come out of your mouth like that?!

Momma deserves to have someone who makes her feel special. And for your information he is more than a bed buddy. He is considerate loving and generous. Maybe if you kill the attitude and get to know him, you would feel different."

I prayed that my ears were deceiving me. Chanelle was putting a man before me. On that day I knew things would never be the same between us.

My heart stayed heavy for the rest of the day. Momma had hurt me in the worst way. I believe that certain bonds should never be comprised. Especially not because of a man. Me and Chanelle were better than that ...or so I thought.

Sleep was all I could do to contain the pain I was feeling. My dreams were infested with Chanelle's words. All I could remember when I woke up, was falling off a cliff. I looked up as Chanelle dropped me and reached for someone else. The person had no face, but I knew who it was. I know-- this is mad dramatic. But it wouldn't be Toi if it wasn't.

A distraction is definitely what I needed. And the only thing that came to mind was D .

I've decided that I hate pagers .Whoever invented them must have been mad busy. The reason I have a problem with them is simple. All the power belongs to whoever you are paging. Cell phones? Now that's what is up.

Moments later D calls back." Hello?"

All I could hear in the background was noise. "What's up shorty?" Nothing, just thinking about you. Is everything ok?"

I pull the phone away from my ear as D yells "Yo, turn that shit down .Sorry, these niggas ain't got no home training. Naw, I'm cool, Manny's the one fucked up. I'm gonna scoop you up later. That cool?"

Quickly I replied, "Yeah . . . do you know what time?"

"Around twelve, bring some clothes. I'll drop you off at school tomorrow."

"See you later." When I hung up the phone, I thought how easily I was going along with everything D demanded. I wasn't sure if I was feeling lonely or if I was just falling.

Before I knew it twelve o'clock was already here. My mad dash towards the door was interrupted by Mike, "Where are you going and what's up with the bag? Chanelle pissed you off that much."

I looked at him and pushed my way through. "Mike move. I'll see you later. By the way, did Chenelle have time to help you out with your problem?"

Mike started laughing and said, "Yeah, I'm cool."

I looked out the window to see if D was here yet. As I saw him pull up I smiled and thought, this man puts a smile on my face all the time. When I got in the car it was obvious that he had just rolled out of the bed. He was rockin' wrinkled jean shorts, a white wife beater and some crisp white sneakers. I kissed him on the face and said, "It looks like you had a rough night."

D snickered and said, "Yeah, I'm tired as hell. You got a nigga all out of character.

Cursed by the Candy

Getting up all early to pick up some braud, never me. Shit I don't move for nothing unless it's about money .What you doing to me girl?"

Perma-smiles, that's the only way I can describe my expression .We went straight to D's house. I had apricot massage oil, candles the whole works. If my baby wasn't gone yet, he will be after tonight.

The moment we hit the door D was laid out on the couch. "Do you mind if I put my things in the room?"

"Naw, go ahead."

Everything was working out perfectly. I thought, *please no interruptions today.* I went in the room and rubbed my body down with warm vanilla bean lotion and I topped it off with baby oil. I had found this beautiful sheer lingerie set at Victoria's Secret .The moment I saw it I new D would be weak. I looked around to make sure everything was perfect...

I walked through his home like I lived there. It felt so right. I put the oil in the microwave and walked over to him. His eye's were closed and it was obvious he was about to be in another world.

D must have felt my presence because he turned around and said, "Damn girl, you move around like a cat. I almost forgot your ass was here."

I leaned over and offered an apology. "Sorry baby," I said as I sucked on his earlobe. I could feel his body getting weaker by the moment.

"Damn girl, you smell good", is all he could manage to say. I stood up and allowed his eyes to examine my body. "Damn girl, I see you've been busy." His eyes were saying everything that I knew his body was feeling.

I reached for him and said, "Let's go into the room. I want to continue what we started the other night."

I took the oil out and followed D back into the room. I watched as the warm solution trickled down my baby's spine. He began to moan as I blew soft kisses down his back. The deep tissue massage would have his ass crawling up the walls and I knew it.

After about 15 minutes D could no longer take it. He flipped over and pinned me on the bed. "Girl you fucking with my head .Toi, my life is mad crazy. I don't have room to be getting all fucked up in the head over no chick. Staying focused is what my life depends on."

I refused to let this night take a negative turn. This shit was about to cease and right now. Slowly I placed my fingers on his lips and said, "Focus on me".

Our mouths took on lives of their own. And before I knew it D was sliding down my gown. His touch felt so right it was like an outer body experience. My body became a Godiva chocolate and D ate every last bit.

Cursed by the Candy

By the time he entered my body I had cum at least three times. The intensity is definitely something I had never experienced. And a feeling like this has to be once in a lifetime. You better believe after that day I was instantly in love. My mind, body and soul belonged to D and he knew it.

The next morning when I awoke the bed was a lonely place. I called out to D but got no response. As I rolled out of bed I heard the sound of music playing downstairs.

When I approached the kitchen the sight of white powder was spread across the counter. D stood up quickly and met me in the doorway, "Baby, we need to talk. And please understand this is no joke. Anything you hear or ever see around me is between us. My business comes before anything or anyone. Don't get me wrong. I'm feeling you like no other, however I have no problem hurting you or anyone else that interferes with my business." D showed no sign of concern on his face about the perplexed look that I was giving him. He just leaned over and said, "You understand?"

Everything that Riccy had ever said to me was coming back loud and clear. She had tried to warn me. I just kept hearing her voice say, *"Can you handle him girl?"*

My mind was heading in one direction, but my heart was here. I looked up at D and said, "I understand."

As I turned to go back to the room, D stopped me and said, "You wanna go to

Manny's funeral with me?" I stood there and looked at him for a moment before I answered.

The words finally escaped my mouth, "Anything for you baby."

Manny's funeral was the topic of the week. You have to understand a hustler's funeral is serious. It's all about fashion and status .The best club in the world has nothing on a Don's funeral. Females prepare for outings like this. Draped in nothing but the best. Hair laid down to perfection. And all in search of the biggest "Candyman".

Now on the flip side, brothas are on point too. They're trying to be a bit incognito. Scooping out who appears to be out of place and checking out the

Feds checking out them. Either way you look at it everyone has an agenda.

For me the funeral was not all that serious. I just wanted to support D. I had already snagged one of the largest hustlers in VA. But don't get it twisted my radar was in full effect.

Officially this was me and D's first outing together and the vipers were definitely going to be in full effect.

My feelings about attending the funeral with D were torn. I was definitely flattered he asked, but I was scared also .Getting too close too fast can be dangerous .The more time we spent together the more time I began to crave. It was starting to become like an addiction.

D handled his business while I took a bath. When I finished I screamed down the hall, "Baby call me when you're done." In a matter of minutes D was in the room with me.

He pulled me into his arms and said, "Your mine now, remember that. "

I searched his eyes for an entrance, but found none. My heart dropped. I don't know if it was out of fear or what. But the look on his face excited and scared me all at once.

Monday, D dropped me off at school. The moment my feet hit the ground I saw Marquetta and Sharice. My mouth almost hit the floor when I noticed that Marquetta had a cast on her arm. I just wanted to start stepping in the opposite direction, but it was too late. They had already seen me.

My eyes were telling what my heart was feeling. I couldn't even look into the girl's face. I felt straight up bad. Within moments I was approaching Riccy, "Damn, the girl, gets chauffeured around now?!"

I couldn't contain the smile growing on my face. "Don't hate."

Sharice started laughing and said, "You must have had a nice weekend. I was about to report your ass as a missing person. I started thinking about what she said and asked her if Chanelle had called to see about where I was.

"Why did you even say that-- did Chanelle call asking about where I was?" Sharice looked at me like I was crazy. "Toi, what the hell do you think? And she was mad as hell. Her and moms talked for about an hour. And thanks to yo' ass, I was interrogated for about an hour."

My mind had drifted in moments. Then I remembered Marquetta was standing right there. Her expression made it seem like she was feeling out of place. I tried to break the ice, "Hey girl, how are you doing today?" She acted as though she didn't hear me.

She just looked at Sharice and said,"Im about to go to class. I'll see you later." Marquetta just walked away as if I didn't even exist. The tension was obvious.

Sharice looked at me and said, "Damn her ass is acting strange."

All day I could hardly focus on my classes. If I wasn't thinking about D, I was thinking about Chanelle. I'm not going to front , my ass was scared to go home.

I looked up at the clock and thought to myself, *Of all the days to fly by, why in the hell did today have to be one of them?* From that moment on my stomach was in knots. If someone has a momma like mine I know damn well you can relate. She definitely has mad influence over me. Whether I like it or not. And my stomach was feeling all of it .

I was definitely zoning in route to my locker. Before I knew it, I had bumped into this girl.

"You need to watch where the hell you are walking!" This chick had gone all Rambo before I could even apologize. I looked up and noticed it was the bitch that was at my house the other night. Oh hell, she doesn't even know who she is dealing with. Miss Toi's representative came out in full force.

"You obviously don't remember me."

She looked at me like I was crazy and said, "Why would I?"

The more attitude I got from her the more I became motivated to put her ass on blast. "Refresh my memory; were you the chick that was at my house on your knees the other night? You so busy I didn't get a chance to introduce myself. I'm Toi, Mike's sister."

To this day I wished I had a camera .This chick damn near turned white. The look of embarrassment was evident. Normally I would have stayed there a few more minutes just to fuck with her. But in reality my mission had already been accomplished . As I was about to walk away, I swear I couldn't help myself, "By the way you, might want to get checked out, because Mike's dick was about to fall off the other day!"

I sat their wishing she would say another word. At this point it was obvious that my verbal abuse had taken a toll on her for the day. Before I knew it she was walking down the hallway fast as hell. *Shit, that's what her ass gets for acting all hype. Better believe I'm going to have the last word. Always.*

Thank God Chenelle was still at work when I got home.

All I could focus on was the feeling of my bed. The moment I stepped into my bedroom door I noticed a letter on my bed. *Oh shit!* Now realize, my momma doesn't have a lot of time, so for her to actually sit down and write a letter is just unheard of.

Toi,

It's 3oclock in the morning. And I am scared to death that something has happened to you. Luckily my fears were relieved when I noticed that you had taken your personals with you. I'm assuming you had this all planned out. I do realize that I hurt you today and I am women enough to apologize. After that being said, Toi you need to realize that momma has a life too. Disrespect is something that I will not tolerate. Baby, I love you dearly, but you need to make a decision on how you are going to live your like. Freedom is what you earn .We have never had any problems like this before. Respecting me enough as your mother should be the reason you call and let me know your whereabouts. This is something that is not negotiable. Better understand that this is a requirement in order for me to trust you. Call me when you get home …

Love, Momma

Cursed by the Candy

I felt like this letter had taken on a life of its own. And before I knew it the trash can was its new home. I was hardly in the mood for all of this right now. At that moment, D rescued me from all of the drama. When I picked up the phone my heart immediately, melted. "Hello..."

The sound of his deep voice was so relaxing. "Hey you, what's up?"

"Nothing, you must have known I was thinking about you."

"Naw, shorty, I just wanted to let you know I had picked up something for you today." Now you know every woman loves gifts, so this felt like Christmas or something.

"What, baby?"

"Nothing much just some shit this booster had. It's a suit. Something you can wear to the funeral. You still going right?"

"Yeah, of course. Baby thanks a lot. You didn't have to do that; I had something in here I could have worn--"

D cut me off and said, "Toi, you my girl now, so you don't ever have to thank me for shit. Just keep treating me good and I will always take care of you. And after the weekend we just had, there ain't shit you couldn't get from me right about now. Show a nigga respect and keep our business at home, you'll be alright with me. Better believe that."

I was in disbelief from the firmness of his words. I swear I love this man.

"I'm going to drop this off in a little while. That cool?"

A smile was overwhelming my face, "Yeah, that's ok." I had to know this was too damn good. The next words from his mouth made my heart drop. I guess he had this all planned out. Bring me up just to shoot me back down.

"Toi, I'm gonna be busy for the next couple of days. There's some shit that I need to take care of, so I'm going to be ghost for a few". Shit, my hands were tied, what the hell was I supposed to say? So as you know I played my position to the fullest and said, "Alright baby."

An hour later he was knocking at the door. When I laid my eyes on this two-piece black Liz Claiborne suit I almost passed out. You can't even imagine how fierce this suit was. The collar was lined in black mink and the pants fit like they had been tailored just for me. Remember I have an eye for some clothing and I know the real deal from the bullshit. And after carefully inspecting it, I knew he had to whip out at least a grip for this. A booster or not this shit was tight. I hated the fact that I couldn't share this with anyone. But the rules had already been laid out loud and clear. Keep our business between us. And I fully planned on doing that. Trust is everything if not the *only* thing when you're dealing with a hustler. Ladies remember that.

My spirits had been lifted up a bit. Nothing soothes the soul better than some good clothes.

Positive energy was flowing through my veins so I decided to call Chanelle. Might as well get it over with.

"Hey Ma," was all I could think to say when she answered the phone.

"'Hey Ma' hell, Toi. Where the hell have you been?!"

I took a moment to answer, "Ma, I needed a little time to myself."

She just ignored my comment and said, "Get Mike to bring you down here, I need some help." Before I could say another word the dial tone was all in my ear.

The tension between me and Chanelle was obvious the moment I stepped into the shop. The day went by fast. And before I knew it I was side by side with Chanelle in the car.

The ride seemed like it took forever. The Mercedes was filling up with steam from the tension in the car. I decided to break the ice. "Ma, a friend of mind wants me to go to this funeral with him."

Chanelle looked at me and said, "Who died?"

"Just this guy," I said. She looked at me like I was stupid.

"So you're telling me, that you are going to a funeral and you don't even know the person?"

"Dag Ma, I'm just going to support my friend."

Chanelle turned around and said, "Who do you think you're bullshitting? I work in Gossip Central all day long. Why the hell do you think we've been so busy? Because everyone is trying to get ready for the same funeral you're talking about. Tell me if I'm wrong? This drug dealer got killed and this is supposed to be the event of the year."

My ears were burning by the time Chanelle finished I didn't know what to say. So I just looked out of the window.

"And what's this I hear about you riding around with this nigga in a cream colored Jag? I work my ass off all damn day long and can hardly afford this car. So tell me what the hell this young man is doing? Because I swear I need some tips."

Before I even spoke I had already chosen my words carefully. I didn't get a chance to say a word though because she was on a roll and had no intentions of stopping anytime soon.

"He's a drug dealer and I know it. So don't even try and fix your mouth to tell me something different. Toi, I'm going to say this one time and one time only. You come in my house pregnant, you get locked up or anything else behind this boy, you're on your own. I brought you and Mike up better than this. I was once young too. I understand, but you need to use some common sense. Just because momma's not around doesn't mean I don't know what's going on. Shit, I once too was all about the candy. But I decided to get my own. And I have prayed every day that you and Mike would do the same."

When I got home that evening I was beat mentally and physically. Chanelle had really laid it on me hard. But in actuality I got off kinda easy. She could have tried to knock my ass out.

~~~~~

Manny's funeral was Wednesday and I was all set to go. I hadn't seen my baby in days and I was nearly ill. D picked me up and I could hardly keep the drool from seeping out of my mouth. My baby was doing the damn thing. He was wearing a black Armani suit with some black Gucci snake skin shoes. He was definitely representing for the men. He looked as though he should have been gracing the pages of GQ. Now, my man was certainly settin' the tone, but I was hardly looking shabby. I was feeling like Diane Carroll off of "Dynasty".

Anyone who got a glimpse of us would have been instantly envious. Let me tell you, it was serious like that! It was like we we're celebrities and in a way I guess we were-- "Ghetto Celebrities". D owned respect. Niggas might not have liked him, but they respected him. So that instantly gave me respect, but on the flip side that made me also a pawn in the game. The worst way to get at a niggas heart is by hurting it. And every day that we spent together I knew I was starting to become his beat. And after a while the rhythm would just be about me.

Now let me tell you about this damn funeral. Who in the world has valet parking at a funeral? Now at the club you can pay for valet, but here it didn't work like that. If you were not family and I mean immediate, not Ba Ba's cousin's sister's momma from around the way, you had to be momma or daddy then that valet was yours. Believe that. Only people who were getting valet were the Dons or up and coming ones. Even a Money Maker had to park their own shit!

The moment we pulled up we were treated like royalty, red carpet and all. We were escorted to a row of seats. It was like the VIP section. Family on one side and Ballers and Dons on the other. As we took our seats, the spectators were in full effect. Bitches were green with envy. D made it worse when he held my hand. I know it was my imagination, but I could have sworn I heard a gasp.

Once we were comfortable he pulled out a pair of gold trimmed Gazal eye glasses. I swear the outfit was on point from that moment on.

Now you know it wouldn't have been a funeral if some female didn't get all dramatic. One of the girls I had seen Manny with tried to pull the damn boy out of the casket. It was getting almost to the point I couldn't help but laugh. This was just ridiculous. I can guarantee you that 85% of the people in here didn't give a damn about Manny. They just wanted to be seen. And I must confess I was one of them.

The urge to laugh suddenly disappeared when I noticed Manny's twin boys in his mother's arms crying. I briefly closed my eyes and said a short prayer for them. Memories of my childhood suddenly started haunting my mind. I all too well remember the feeling of losing a parent at a young age.

I was about their age when my daddy died.

The service was coming to an end and everyone stood to begin to leave. The moment I stepped out of the church doors an eerie feeling took over my soul. People were standing around and socializing, you would have thought this was the club or something. I peered out into the crowd. Hoochie Mamas were in full effect today. The clothing and the hairstyles they were rocking were off the hook. It was all a total spectacle. D had walked away for a moment and I was standing alone. Then out of nowhere one of his stalkers approached me.

She walked towards me with a confidence that was to be reckoned with. Now don't get confused, no bitches will every catch me off guard so I'm always prepared. I had to turn around and count back to ten because this particular bitch was about to get on my nerves.

Once I had composed myself, I smiled and extended my hand, "Nice to meet you, what did you say your name was?"

"Desiree," she replied.

"OH, forgive me. I'm so terrible with names. And to respond to your last comment that you I *know* I heard walkin' by-- I'm hardly tagging along with D. We are here together…Is that a problem?"

I swear I saw her eye's turn red. The sister girl's neck movement started to become a distraction. Desiree was about to take this situation into ghetto overload.

"In fact it is a problem, since I just fucked him two days ago!"

Now I'm good at holding back emotions, but this bitch had just struck a nerve. I was pissed that I had even allowed her to touch an emotion. Was it the words that she spit out or the fact that I hadn't seen D in two days? Either way, something in my gut told me she was telling the truth. But, best believe she would never know I didn't doubt her. I just looked her dead in the eye and said, "I hope it was good."

I had enough of this bullshit for the day. I turned around in search of D. He must have noticed the confrontation and was on his way in my direction.

"Are you ready to go?" Were the words that greeted him.

He looked around and said, "Give me a minute, babe..." D stared over at Desiree and then said, "Come here, Toi."

We walked over towards a group of females and D took full control, "Hey Dez, what's up?" All of the confidence she held a moment ago had disappeared. "I saw you talking to my girl and I wanted to officially introduce you to her."

She looked like she wanted to smack the shit out of him. It was funny to me though how home girl had turned into a child that quick. She looked up and said, "Nice meeting you."

I stood their thinking, *What the hell is going on here?* It was like the Twilight Zone. My baby had mad control over everyone. I love him, but I refuse to be anyone's damn puppet. Fuck that!

D walked away for a moment and gave me the ticket for the valet. All of a sudden the crowed started moving. I turned around and saw three masked men hanging out of a car spraying the crowed with bullets. D came out of nowhere and pushed me behind a tree and yelled, "GET DOWN!"

Next thing I knew, him and about five other guys had started shooting back. I put my hands over my head and started praying. I could not believe this was happening-- and at a damn funeral.

A few minutes later everything started to calm down. People were crying and walking fast. I stood up and couldn't find D anywhere. I could feel a panic attack about to kick in. I had no clue what to do, so I just started walking towards the lot where the car was parked.

Police and ambulances started to arrive. I looked around when I heard someone calling my name. Still I saw no familiar face. The crowd was so thick I felt like I was about to suffocate .Within seconds I saw D coming towards me. My heart skipped a beat and the tears started falling. D hugged me tight and said, "Don't cry baby, I'm sorry. Let's get out of here."

The drive was extremely quiet. I didn't know what to say. But I knew not to ask a lot of questions. I looked over at him and noticed he was so calm, like nothing had ever happened. Finally after a few moments he spoke, "Toi you want me to drop you off or you want to go to the hotel with me?"

I was confused about the hotel. "Hotel? Why are you going to a hotel?"

He continued to look straight and said, "I just need to lay low for a couple of days." I knew if I stayed out all night again Chanelle would have a damn cow.

"Yeah, I'll go for a little while. Do you mind dropping me off a little later?" Naw, that's cool.

We pulled up into the Airport Hilton and D got a suite for three days. When we finally got into the room, I couldn't help but feel the mood was all off. But don't get me wrong I fully understood. His boy did just get blasted and to make matters worse someone tried to shoot up the funeral. That was a lot for anyone to take. I tried to break the ice, so I asked D to come lay down beside me. His pager went off and he said, "In a minute, Toi. Let me return this call."

I laid down and started to reflect on the events of the day. My gut was telling me to get out now, but my heart wouldn't let me. D came back into the room and we talked for hours that night. He shared stories about his childhood and family. He opened up a lot that evening. I don't know if it was the adrenaline rush or if he just needed to vent. Either way he had all of my attention.

The more he spoke the more I began to realize how much I had become apart of his life. He was starting to become comfortable enough to let his guard down.

Those precious moments we spent together that night were magical. I learned a lot about D. He had come up from a long history of hustlers. His uncles, cousins and dad were in the game. D's daddy was the "ultimate" Don in his day. He ran the streets of Virginia like a king and was respected in that manner too. My baby's daddy was called Don Don because he was at the top of his game. That's where D received his name Don Don, Jr.

D's daddy was removed from this earth in the late 70s. Gunned down on the block by some jealous wanna-bes. But that's the nature of the game "survival of the sweetest."

~~~~~

Time had gone by fast and before I knew it 10:30 was already here.

He was resting so peacefully I didn't want to disturb him. Just the thought of me having to leave had me all upset. Slowly I kissed him and whispered, "Baby I need to go."

The funeral really had my nerves bad .The sounds of shooting and screaming still rang loud in my ears. And that bitch Desiree really struck a nerve. The urge to ask him about it was overwhelming. But really, what was the point?

He handled it the way he felt fit and I refuse to become a nagger. The more I thought about it the more I felt an urge to start tripping. *Snap out of it Toi, you're better than that!* It just boils down to how I plan on handling the situation. Me and D are fairly new and I'm not trying to rock the boat right now. A gate keeper has never been my occupation and I don't plan on being that now either.

D rolled over and broke my thoughts. He began sucking on my breast like a nursing child. "Mmm, baby, don't stop," I moaned. Needless to say my feet did not hit Chanelle's porch until 2:30 am the next morning. Luck must have been on my side though because Chanelle wasn't home.

I walked upstairs and my bed was awaiting my arrival with opened arms. All I wanted to do that night was sleep and forget about the events of today. Unfortunately my brother had other things on his mind. I was awakened bright and early to a million questions.

"Toi ,what's going on with you and Chanelle?" Just hearing Chanelle's name brought my mood down.

I rolled over and asked him, "Why are you all in my business anyway?! What's up with you ... and Chanelle?" Mike looked stunned by my aggression towards him.

He stood up and said, "Ok Ms. Smartass you think you're grown now, hanging out all times of the night? Who am I going to have to bail out next time?"

I could feel the blood starting to boil. Before I knew what happened I was yelling, "Get out Mike!"

Mike turned to leave and then suddenly stopped, "Chanelle and Riccy called, they wanted to see if you still lived here."

The moment Mike left the room I wanted to cry. Chanelle, D and even school were starting to get to the best of me.

~~~~~

The next day when I went to school, Manny's funeral was the topic of conversation. People acting all emotional, like they even knew him. Half of these bitches didn't even know who he was. That's the thing that aggravates me about people, always trying to make themselves important. The events of school had me all emotional. I found out that one of my classmates was shot at the funeral. I stood by my locker just thinking how easily that could have been me.

You never know what life has in store for you. Being in the wrong place at the wrong time could cause your life to change forever.

My mind was still in deep thought as I walked down the hall. The moment I looked up I saw Marquetta coming in my direction .Just looking at her made me feel bad as hell.

"Hey Toi, I haven't seen you around lately. You and D must be kicking it hard. Huh?" Her comment instantly took my emotional status to another level. And let's just say it was not heading in a good direction. The momentary empathy that I was feeling had now been replaced with anger. I stood there looking at her for a moment before I decided it was not that serious. Shit, I have more important things to be thinking about.

Finally I realized I had not seen my cousin all day so I decided to ask her, "Have you seen Riccy around today?"

Marquetta started to walk away and said, "No, I don't think she's here today." Her expression suddenly changed as she spoke. "Toi, I just wanted you to know I saw you and D the other night...thanks..." She started to walk away and I felt the urge to explain, but I decided against it. Shit what was I supposed to do?! This is a perfect example of why I don't mess with females. I stood their thinking, *I can't wait for this day to be over.* I sure the hell didn't want to bump into her again.

The moment I walked in the door the phone began to ring. "Hello," I said as I tried to lay my bags down.

"What's up girl?" Riccy was on the other end speaking very low.

"Why didn't you come to school today?"

"Girl I have the flu or something, but I didn't call to talk about me. You know I'm mad at your ass. Where have you been? Chanelle and my momma have been interrogating me and shit! What's going on with you?"

Cursed by the Candy

I was about to speak when Riccy cut me off, "Toi, please be careful. I heard you went to the funeral with D. That girl he used to mess with is crazy over that nigga. I think her name is Desiree or something like that. She lives in those projects over by Norfolk State. They say her stupid ass is being a "mule" for him. He had her doing all kinds of crazy shit.

Everything in my soul wanted to defend him. I paused a moment in search for the correct words. "Thank you for the information Riccy. But I know damn well D better not ever ask me to do some shit like that. And, as far as Ms.Desiree is concerned, D dealt with her yesterday."

I heard Sharice sighing and probably thinking I was full of shit. The silence was finally broken and just in time.

"All right girl, just watch yourself. The candy down south may have a whole different flava."

I felt my body getting angrier every second I stayed on the phone. "Well, let me go and do some work around here girl. I hope you feel better." I don't know who I thought I was fooling. Sharice knows me all too well.

She started coughing and said, "Don't be mad, just be careful."

Deep down I knew everything she was saying was true. But now it was too late.

Cursed by the Candy

I could have walked in on him with the girl and probably felt the same about him. It's funny how love can warp the strongest woman's mind. Every day I was becoming a stranger to myself. But I didn't care. I knew there was no turning back now. And honestly I didn't want to.

My day had already been messed up. So I decided to call Chanelle and get the drama out of the way. I thought I had dialed the wrong number when I heard a male voice on the other end, "For Diva's Only," he said. An instant attitude emerged through my veins. I know good and damn well he didn't just answer the phone! Caring about his feelings was the least of my concerns. I didn't even try and hide the anger in my voice.

"Can I speak to my mother please?!"

Charles paused for a moment and said, "Is everything all right?" The sound of his voice made me ill.

I just ignored his pleasantries. "Is Chanelle there?" Charles paused for a moment and said, "Hold on a minute, baby." If someone was around they would have been laughing at my facial expression, *Baby, who the hell is he calling baby?*

A moment later Chanelle came on the phone. I felt like hanging up, all the desire I once felt to speak with her was now gone.

"Hello," she said.

"Hey Ma, how are you doing?" The noise in the shop was so loud I could hardly make out what she was saying.

"Toi, I'm going to have to call you back later. I am extremely busy today. You ok?"

I couldn't say a word, I just hung up the phone.

My emotional state of mind was all over the place. Five minutes later the phone was ringing. "Hello?"

I had to move the phone away from my ear so I wouldn't go deaf. Chanelle was going ballistic. "I know damn well you didn't just hang up on me!"

I started stuttering trying to explain myself, "M-M-Ma, I'm sorry it was an accident, d-didn't want to call back and disturb you. Are you coming home tonight?" There was silence in the phone so I said, "Are you there, Ma?"

Chanelle came back to the phone and said, "Toi what did you say?" I swear this woman is about to drive me crazy today."

"I saaaaid, *are you coming home tonight?* We don't have anything in here to eat!" The moment my tone of voice rose I knew I was in trouble.

In a stern tone Chanelle said, "You raise your voice at me one more time I will come home and we can finish this conversation!" Lawd, why did I get her started? I was about to try and cut in, but she cut me off in the middle of my sentence.

"Get Mike to bring you up here." And before I could say another word the dial tone was in my ear. "Bye Ma...."

~~~~~

My week was real quiet and boring as hell. Chanelle was doing her thing and Sharice was still sick. I had paged D for a couple of days and still he had not called me back. My woman's intuition was telling me something was wrong. Saturday rolled around and I was sad as hell. All of the bad memories of PJ start coming back. Please don't let me go through that again. My heart just couldn't take it. At this point sleep became my best friend.

Saturday morning rolled around and the demons had definitely taken over. I had even considered going over to the hotel room. But for what? To be embarrassed? I already knew what was going on. And I couldn't even believe I was tripping like this.

The sound of a car door broke my thoughts. *Damn probably some of those Jahova Witness's trying to hustle there Watch Tower Books.*

A tree was blocking my view so I ran downstairs. The moment I hit the stairs D was walking back towards his car. All of the feelings of anger I was holding disappeared the moment I saw him. I opened the door and he came back.

"Hey you," he said with his smooth talk.

I leaned up against the railing and said, "Oh you decided to make an appearance?"

D licked his lips and said, "Naw, shorty, it's not like that. I had some business to take care of."

One of my rules was about to be broken, but I didn't care. I looked at him with a sincere expression and said, "Baby, I was worried." To my surprise he just changed the subject and acted like I hadn't said a word.

He pushed the hair out of my face and said, "What's up for this weekend? Let's roll to DC."

I stood their in shock thinking I will not allow this nigga to run over me. "D I'm not trying to start an argument, but I asked you a question. Don't ignore me like that!" Aggravation was written all over his face, but I didn't give a shit.

He rubbed his hands over his head and said "Damn Toi, why you interrogating me like that!?" I was over all the bullshit so I just backed down.

"D, just forget it!"

We sat there for what seemed like forever. Finally D grabbed me by the arm and said "Stop all that damn whining." I just melted in his arms and inhaled his strong cologne. I stood there with my head on his shoulder. He whispered in my ear, "Baby, I just had some stuff to take care of. I know that shit Desiree said to you hit a nerve. But if we are going to be together you have to let that bullshit ride."

The tension from my body felt like it had been lifted. I was glad it was all out in the open for now. But my intuition still had me on high guard. I knew from past experiences that this was hardly over.

The ride to DC was definitely what I needed. Just being with D made me feel better. We stopped in Williamsburg and went shopping at one of the outlet malls. My baby must have had some things on his mind because the whole trip he barley whispered a word.

On our way back to the car I stopped in the middle of the road and pulled him close to me, "Baby are you ok? You have barley said a word to me all day.

D grabbed one of my bags that I had placed on the ground and said, "Baby everything is cool." I start thinking he was feeling guilty. I enjoyed the trip and everything, but it was obvious that he was lying about his whereabouts this week. Ladies I may be a little bit gone, but I am hardly stupid. D was fucking and I know it. However, I do realize that he had chicks before he met me, so I will just give him a few minutes to weed them out. But don't get it twisted though my patience is starting to wear thin. Too much disrespect will have Toi in search of another candy supplier with the quickness.

Any time spent with D is always enjoyable, but the shopping spree, I am sad to say, was the highlight of the weekend. I don't feel like I had D's full attention. He slept the majority of the time and complained about his head hurting. All of my attempts were exhausted. The deep tissue massage, warm bath and foot rub did nothing to relieve his "headache".

"Baby, how long have you been having these headaches?" D rolled over and put the pillow over his head. I didn't want to seem like I nag, but he was not going to ignore me. "D, I know you heard me! Baby stop acting like that."

Finally he flipped over and started talking.

"Dang girl, what..are you a doctor now? I don't know about six or seven months." I know damn well he didn't just say six or seven months.

"You need to go see about that before I'll be rushing you to the hospital."

He started laughing and said, "I didn't know I had two mommas." I looked at him as though he had lost his mind.

"Whatever, you just need to go and handle that."

I laid my head on his chest so I could hear his strong heartbeat. The rhythm always put me at ease. I had never met any of D's family and come to think about it he never has mentioned them either.

"Baby, why don't you ever talk about your mother?"

He looked down at me and said, "What's there to talk about? -- She's a crack head. Enough said." His response had me feeling uneasy .That's Toi for ya, always in someone's business. Now I'm sitting here feeling all stupid. I thought, *what would be the appropriate thing to say now?* Probably nothing. I decided to mind my business and try to enjoy the rest of our trip. I figure he will open up to me in his own time.

The moment we pulled into the driveway my stomach was all in knots. Chanelle will probably be on me the moment I walk into the house. The story I came up with was stupid. I didn't even try to make it sound good. I just wanted to get out of there.

Nope-- I would have to face the consequences. The moment my foot hit the hallway I ran right into her.

"Damn Toi, watch where you are going. You're out of school next Friday right?" I was taken aback by her demeanor.

"I think so why?" She walked into her room so I followed her.

Cursed by the Candy

She sat down on the bed and said, "The shop in Boston is having a hair show next weekend and we are going. I need to get out of here…I am already late .We'll talk about this later." I knew there was no need to object, I was going whether I wanted to or not.

~~~~~

D and I were inseparable all week. He took me to school everyday and picked me up like clockwork. The moment I got in the car I felt the mood was uneasy, but I needed to let him know I was going to Boston this weekend.

I tried to break the ice with a bit of small talk, "Baby how are you feeling today?"

He looked over at me and said, "Ok mommy." That was just like my D to make a joke out of everything. There wasn't any need to continue procrastinating.

"Baby I forgot to tell you I have to go out of town this weekend with Chanelle."

D looked over at me with a blank stare before he spoke, "So, how long have you known about this? I could hear the aggravation in his voice so I decided to lie." Chanelle just told me about it, baby." D's silence was starting to drive me crazy. Flash backs of PJ started running through my mind.

Finally D spoke, "Toi, you remember those ID's you told me about, where did you get them from?" I started wondering, *what in the world does this have to do with anything?* His body language was starting to make me feel uncomfortable so I tried to come up with an answer and quick.

"This guy from Boston named PJ." D's whole demeanor changed; I felt like he was talking to one of his associates on the street. This was a side of him I was unfamiliar with.

In a firm tone he said, "You think he could hook me up?" I looked at him with a questioning expression.

"Baby, I'm not sure, I would have to call him." All of this talking about PJ was making me feel uncomfortable. I felt like I needed to explain myself or something. "D, I want you to know that me and PJ were together when I lived up north."

D just casually looked at me and said, "Toi, this has nothing to do with us, this is about business. See what you can do."

The coldness of his voice made my insides turn .This was not the man I knew. D was a totally different person when it came down to his business. But after getting over the shock of his attitude, I realized this was all a part of the game. And if I wanted to be a player I had to go with the flow.

The moment I went into the house I was in search of PJ's number. Lawd I never in a million years thought I would be calling him again. My stomach began to churn as I stared at the number. Finally I got up enough strength to page him.

Ten minutes later the phone began to ring. "Yo, somebody page me?" He asked.

I cleared my throat and said, "Damn you forgot about a sister already?"

PJ started laughing and said, "Damn Toi what's up girl?" I was amazed at how excited he sounded. "I didn't think I would ever hear from you again." I sat there thinking, *me either*.

After a few minutes of small talk, I finally got up the nerve to ask him. "PJ, I need a favor."

His smooth voice came across the phone line and he said, "Anything for you girl. Just say the word." I ignored his comment and tried to focus on the business at hand.

"Do you still have the hook up to get those ID's?"

PJ paused a moment and said, "Damn girl you lost yours already?" I tried to come up with the best way to ask him without going through a lot of drama.

"No, it would be for someone else. This guy I know." PJ's voice began to escalate and I knew I had hit a nerve.

"Toi, stop fucking around with me and speak your mind. I don't have time to be playing no damn games!" I was also getting tired of this little game we had started to play.

"Ok, PJ my man need's them." I braced myself because I knew he was pissed.

"Toi, I can do something for $3000.00 they are $1500.00 a piece."

I almost chocked on my spit, "$1500.00! Damn PJ, they cost that much?!" My phone started beeping and I wanted to answer it, but I had to take care of this business.

"Hell yeah-- especially for some nigga I don't even know. And also you need to get me two passport pictures." D needed these bad so I agreed.

"That's cool. Me and Chenelle will be down there this weekend. I'll page you once I get settled in. PJ can be shiesty sometimes when things don't go his way. And the last thing I wanted him to do was be ghost once I got down there. "PJ don't mess around, I really need you to come through for me."

PJ started laughing and said, "Damn girl I must say you have always been down for your nigga. And I give you much respect for that. And besides this way I will be able to see your pretty ass." I thought to myself *he must be crazy*. I have hardly developed amnesia since I have been down here.

"PJ please don't make me laugh, you didn't feel that way when you were fucking around on me."

He couldn't contain his laughter anymore he just said, "Truce, shorty, don't get all bent out of shape." This conversation was making me exhausted.

"Alright, I'll call you when I get up there-- bye." When I hung up I felt a headache coming on. I was ashamed that I still allowed him to get to me like that.

I hung up the phone but still held thoughts of PJ on my mind. The fact that I would have to share the same space with him for any amount of time had me bugging. I needed to let my baby know what was up. D's not an emotional type of person, but I'm still worried about how he is going to react to the whole PJ situation.

Before I could even get a chance to call him my phone was ringing. "Hello." D's voice pierced my ears like a knife.

"Toi. Did you talk to that nigga up north?" I was taken back by his aggressiveness, but I just answered his question.

"Yeah, he said it would be $1500 a piece and you would need passport pictures."

D was quiet for a moment then said, "Cool, I'll bring you the money later. And get some stuff together for tonight." I didn't even have a chance to speak before he hung up the phone.

I stared at the phone for a while before the annoying buzzing sound rang through my ears. D is trying to have Chanelle kill me for real.

~~~~~

Midnight came around and D was sitting in the driveway. I was grateful that Chanelle had left with Charles earlier.

The moment I stepped into the car, I felt tension. D is normally quiet, but tonight something was different. We sat in silence the entire time. When we entered the house I reached for his hand and said, "Baby what's wrong?"

He sat silent for a minute before he grabbed me around the neck and said, "Toi if you give my pussy away I will kill you!" I tried to break away from his embrace, but the more I struggled the tighter his grip became. When he finally let go I was gasping for air. I fell to the floor like a puddle of water.

The silence was violently interrupted by his yelling, "GET UP," he said. As I stood up I tried to fight back the tears.

"Why are you acting like this?! I have never given you a reason not to trust me."

D stood before me in the dark. A demon had taken my baby to another place that night and I didn't know what to do. Finally he spoke and a chill ran down my spine. "I can't stand the thought of another man touching you. If I didn't need this shit I would tell you to fuck it!"

The rain drops on the skylight had my body hypnotized. I stared into D eyes gathering up enough strength to engage in my next move. All I wanted was for this day to expire. I craved the connection that we had started to create. Finally I placed my hands on D's face and said, "Baby... my heart belongs to you. There's nothing I wouldn't do for us... Please don't ever doubt me again."

Our kisses and tears mixed together. Then I heard the words like an echoing in my soul, "Toi I love you." My body felt like it was drowning in a pool of lust and emotions. All I wanted was to feel the love D spoke of within my walls of honey. We made love all night long as the words flowed off my tongue…"I love you too baby."

Chapter 5

Bright and early the next morning me and Chanelle were on our way to Boston. My body was on the plane, but my thoughts were still in bed with D. I had planned on sleeping the entire trip, but my dreams were interrupted — I opened my eyes and looked over at Chanelle, "What's wrong?"

Chanelle took off her glasses and replaced them with eyes of a cat. Slowly she began to speak, "Everything is wrong, Toi .You have totally changed since we moved to Virginia."

I tried my hardest to contain my frustration. I was certainly not in the mood for a heart to heart this damn early in the morning. She must have felt the negative vibe because she picked up her book and left me alone. I should have known her response was too good to be true because five minutes later the questions began to flow again. I sat their thinking to myself, *damn can I get a moment of peace*? I looked out the window and tried to find the tranquility that I thought the clouds would provide. But Chanelle was breathing down my back and made the scenery seem like the worst storm.

I felt the warm embrace of her hand as she looked at me the way only a mother could and said, "Baby talk to me, what's going on?" I pulled my hand away and focused on the largest cloud I could find.

Cursed by the Candy

Staring was the only thing I could do to keep the tears from falling. Before D came into my life, Chanelle was my world, my best friend. But the cycle of my life has changed now and so has the bond we once shared. I locate my earphones and placed them on my head with a cautionary attitude. I still did realize that Chanelle would embarrass me quickly.

I found some peace behind the curtains of my eyelids. I smiled at her and said, "Everything is fine, Ma."

The moment I stepped off the plane the cold northern air hit me like it had a personal gripe with me. The memories of my past life started to suffocate me. .Just the thought of me laying my eyes on PJ again made my skin feel warm.

But not in a good way. D had become my pulse and there was nothing that I wouldn't do for him. Even if it meant me sharing the same space with PJ for a moment.

The hotel room had a warm feeling to it which calmed my nerves immediately. Laughter broke my thoughts as I heard Chanelle in the bathroom. Obviously Charles had been on her mind just as much as D had been occupying my thoughts.

Finally Chanelle vacated the bathroom and I went in to freshen up a little before PJ got here. Moments later I heard keys jingling and Chanelle's voice became a distant memory. "Toi, I'm going out, I'll see you later."

So much for our bonding period I thought. But who am I kidding? -- I wasn't down for all that anyway. The phone seemed like a foreign objected in my hand. My mind was saying dial the number, but my body was saying let me go back into the bathroom. I wiped my hands across my face and took a deep breath, "Come on Toi stop being so dramatic."

I called PJ and an hour later he was sitting in the lobby. I inspected myself in the elevator door trying not to look too sexy. But knowing PJ I could have had on some pajamas and he would have taken it there. As soon as the elevator stopped the butterflies took over. The threshold of the elevator damn near had me lying on my face. *Dang, that sure did bring back memories.* Only PJ could have me acting like a clumsy fool.

I spotted him immediately sitting in the lounge chair with a ray of respect all over his body. One thing about PJ, he always gave off that vibe, big time. I approached him slowly, but better believe he knew I was there. A major characteristic of a hustler is being observant, always.

"Hey, Mr. Jackson," I said in the best homey voice I could come up with. He turned around and smiled.

"Damn Toi, VA must be treating you good… or your man is." I ignored his comment and tried to stay focused.

A strange feeling came across me all of a sudden. I could swear we were being watched. Who knows what kind of mess Pj might be in by now? Maybe he felt it also, because he said in a rushed manner, "Toi let's take this outside to the car."

The cold air almost took my breath away. I looked towards PJ for directions towards the car .The next thing I knew the valet was pulling up a brand new GS300 Lex. I smiled in his direction and said, "I see you have upgraded."

PJ grabbed my face and said, "If you had been acting correct you could have been pushing the BM."

I pushed his hand away and said, "Whatever." I glanced at the car quickly,

I sure wasn't about to give him no more bragging rights. *Fuck that!* I'm going to act like this is a damn Pinto. PJ is already arrogant enough; he definitely doesn't need any more fuel.

Since I had moved down South, Boston seemed so cramped now. Everything was so close and congested I felt like I couldn't breathe. My throat felt dry and the words barley would come out, but I managed, "PJ where is the stuff?" He looked in his rearview mirror and acted as though no words had even left my lips.

So I spoke again but, louder, "PJ I know you heard me."This time I got his attention, but I certainly was cautious. He squinted his face up and looked at me like I was crazy.

"Damn girl, what you in a rush for? Give a nigga a minute. You bring the shit I told you to?" I pulled out the pictures and the money. PJ glanced at the picture and said, "We going to have to go down to Roxbury so I can do this."

Instantly I started having flashbacks of the incident with Tanya. I swear it causes me nightmares every now and then. Shit, I sure the hell ain't trying to call it quits this early in my life. Next thing I knew the words were coming out, "PJ, Im not trying to be up in this car with you for real." He hit the break so hard I swear I almost flew out the window.

"Damn Toi stop wasting my valuable time. Better believe I am losing some paper out here trying to help yo' ass out!

What you want to do." I was sinking and fast-- I had to tell him something. We were in a race of words and I lost.

PJ started speaking again, "Look, just give me the dough and shit and I'll bring the stuff back to you later." My face felt like it was about to mutate into another figure.

"Are you crazy? I'm not giving you this man's money without the IDs!"

My heart skipped a beat when PJ pulled over towards an abandoned building. He got out of the car and came over to my side. I swear I didn't know what to do. I tried to lock the door real quick, but he was too fast. He opened the door and pulled me out by my coat.

Cursed by the Candy

"First up, who the fuck you think you talking to?! Those niggas down south got your head blown up like that. Bitch you better fall back into position and quick! You need this shit not me. Toi, I make $3g's an hour. Yo' nigga's money don't mean shit to me. You better be glad I still have love for you or your ass would be splattered all over this ground. Get yo' silly ass back into the car and stop wasting my time!"

I followed his direction quickly. My hands were shaking so bad I could hardly keep them still. I felt like an idiot. D got my head all fucked up. I forgot my own rules RESPECT ALWAYS!

All the drama I caused was so unnecessary. PJ was in and out in a flash. He got in the car and threw an envelope in my lap. He said in a fatherly stern manner, "Don't make it a habit telling my business to those down south niggas!"

I was so embarrassed all I could do was apologize. "PJ Im sorry I was tripping." I knew PJ still cared about me so I knew my apology would be accepted no doubt.

He looked at me and said, "You want something to eat?" My mouth almost got me in trouble again. Eating was the last thing I wanted to do, but it certainly would have been an insult if I would have said no.

All in all I was glad I went to lunch with him. It was sort of closure to a chapter that had been opened too long. PJ told me he had a son on the way. I must admit I was a bit bothered for a moment, but it passed quickly. He deserved to be happy and I was glad for him. Till this day I will never forget the taste of that sweet northern love.

We got back to the hotel and said our last good byes. PJ looked at me as though this could be our last encounter and as if he knew it would be. "Toi, that nigga got you opened like that? Look at me and tell me my love don't still flow through your veins." His words were deep and scary. I knew it was time to make my exit. I certainly would not be able to take this much longer.

I plastered a smile on my face and said in a sweet tone, "PJ, you will always flow through my veins like a hot river that caused my heart to hurt. You brought me sadness and pain that I can hardly explain. You were my first love and I will always remember you for that. I can't say I don't still care for you because I always will. At one point you were my exsistance before I even knew what I existed for. You were my love and definitely my first "Candy Man"."

PJ sat their looking crazy for a minute. He started laughing and then said, "Toi what the hell is a Candy Man?" I bent over and kissed him softly on the cheek.

The words caressed his ears like the the softest song never heard, "You baby ...A hustler with street credibility and dough flowing from all ends. A man who demands respect and gets it from everyone. A brotha with confidence like a King so therefore he is treated that way." PJ takes a deep breath and stares out the window. Finally his attention is directed back to me. He snickers a bit then says, "Candy Man, damn Toi I like that."

I have always hated long drawn out goodbyes and it was time to wrap this up. I grabbed for the handle and PJ stopped me. "Toi I swear if you ever need anything and mean anything, call me." I appreciated the gesture of love, but I knew our paths would never cross again.

I pulled his hand towards my lips and placed on it the sweetest kiss ever imagined and then said, "Thank you."

As I walked back into the hotel I felt a sense of pride. I was proud that I did not allow PJ to enter my world again. The love I have for D cannot be measured in any manner. Love was an understatement when it came to what we had.

The moment I stepped my foot back in the hotel Chanelle was on me like a hawk. "Damn Toi where have you been?" I walked over to the window and glanced at the beautiful skyline Boston had to offer. It's so funny how the little details mean so much. Shit, a skyline down south is unheard of. My attention was immediately redirected back to Chanelle's inquires.

"Ma, I went to get something to eat. Why, what's wrong?" She looked over at the clock and said, "What's wrong is that our plane is leaving in an hour."

A confused expression took over my face. "An hour, why are we going back already?"

Chanelle grabbed her eye glasses and said "Girl just get your stuff together. The hair show was cancelled." I swear I can't tell you how that was like music to my ears. I couldn't wait to get back to my baby.

Before Chanelle could say another word my stuff was ready and waiting. Shit, all the motivation I needed was laying my eyes back on D. The moment we got to the airport I called Riccy to see if she could pick us up. I swear it seemed like the phone was ringing for about an hour before she finally answered," Hello", her voice pierced the air like she was aggravated.

"Damn girl what took you so long?"

Immediately her mood lightened when she heard my voice, "Hey Toi, where are you?"

"In Boston trying to get back to VA .Can you pick me and Chanelle up at the airport?"

Riccy paused and said, "What time?" Thinking to myself, *damn what's the problem?*

"Around 9:30, you have something to do tonight?"

She started laughing and said, "No we have something to do tonight".

I swear I hate word games. "You act like I'm not calling long distance. Hurry up and spit it out."

"Oh, damn girl I'm sorry. We going to Magic's tonight. You down?" Clubbing was the last thing on my mind tonight. I just wanted to be with D. But knowing his ass he would probably be up in there anyway.

"Yeah I'll go. D will probably be in their tonight. So I'll surprise him. He thinks I'm not coming back until Sunday." I heard a soft sigh on the phone which caused me to have an immediate attitude, "What's all that huffing and puffing about?"

Riccy detected my attitude right off the bat and said, "Nothing girl, your ass is paranoid as hell when it comes down to that nigga! Can a sista breathe?" I started thinking *she must think I'm stupid; I know what I heard.* "But anyway later for that. I'll just see you at that airport, ok." I hung up the phone and had an irritated vibe coming over me.

Damn maybe she's right, am I paranoid? The flight wasn't going to board for another 20 minutes so I decided to page D. Chanelle was about to have a cow so I had to go and stand in line. Fifteen minutes had passed and D still hadn't called back. The moment I sat down in the seat thought started coming from all directions. Good ones, bad ones-- I just couldn't focus. I started thinking about the last time me and D were together everything was just so intense. Before I knew it, we were landing at Norfolk International Airport.

Sharice was there and prompt as usual. I gave her a quick sista girl hug and said, "What's going on, what time are we going out tonight?" The moment the words came I regretted it.

"Going out? I don't remember you asking could you go any damn where." Chanelle was on a roll now.

"Jesus give me a break." Riccy sat there looking crazy because she knew Chanelle was about to get on a role. I tried to diffuse the situation immediately because if Chenelle kept at it, I would be sitting right home looking stupid. "Ma, I'm sorry I thought I asked you the other day. Do you mind if I go out with Riccy tonight?"

Chanelle looked at me and said, "You know damn well you didn't ask if you could go out. And I should say no because your trying to make me think I'm stupid! You sure are becoming Little Miss Liar. Are you really going out with her?"

Sharice intercepted just in time, "Auntie Chanelle, I asked her earlier this week. We're going to this little teen club."

Chanelle laughed and said, "Teen my foot, you ladies forget me and your mama were once young too. Toi, if you go out tonight you will be glued to the shop for the rest of the week. You hear me?!" At this point I didn't care;

Cursed by the Candy

anything I had to do to get to D was minor. She kills me acting all concerned now, as soon as we get home I will become nonexistent again and she will be all up in Charles's face.

The moment I got home my fingers was itching to call D. But something stopped me in the middle of the number. I guess you call it that female intuition. A tingle in my spine had me feeling that something was going on.

~~~~~

The air felt still and a chill touched my bones as I got out of the car. Magic's was packed tonight, row to row cars. Brotha's everywhere. The back parking lot was off the hook. We hardly could find a spot, but Ms. Riccy worked her magic with security and got us up front. *That's my girl.* Ballers of all variety were in the house tonight. Sharice touched my arm and pointed to D's car. "See you were right, he is in here tonight." Normally I would have been instantly excited, but for some reason tonight I wasn't.

My night already had an uneasy vibe to it. The moment I stepped into the club Marquetta was the first face I saw. *Lawd, not tonight, I thought.* See this is exactly why I don't mess with chicks, just too much damn drama. Riccy embraced her with a hug and as I was about to show some manners and speak she rolled her eyes at me and walked away.

Sharice caught on quick and said, "What the hell was that about and where was I when all this animosity started?" Ignoring her was all I could think to do. I refused to give this bitch any of my energy tonight.

I looked a Riccy and said, "Don't worry about it."

She looked pissed and said, "Don't worry about it?! My good friend is tripping out on my fam and no one will tell me what is going on?" All of the extra unnecessary commotion was getting on my nerves. I had to get a drink and quick.

I leaned against the bar and observed the atmosphere. It's amazing what you see when you just sit back and observe. The normal eye would just witness nice dressed ballers flossing jewels and seeking the attention of their fans. But I viewed things totally differently. I see strong black men from the street trying to find respect from their peers. Women with self esteem issues who are in search for materials that a hustler can provide to boost their esteem. It's amazing to me the power of Candy in one's life. It can break down the strongest mind and soul. Me on the other hand I don't know what category I fall into. I would have never thought I had esteem issues until I meet D. Now I find myself questioning my every move and my worth in regards to this man. It happened so abruptly, I hardly realized it until now.

I focused my attention towards the pool table and that's when I saw D. My heart took a break for a moment. This is exactly what I'm talking about, *Come back Toi*.

I was about to approach him, but then I decided to chill for a moment. About five minutes passed when I saw Desiree all up in his face, but what made it unbearable is the fact that he seemed to be enjoying it. Over the past few months I have learned his body language, what makes him tick what makes him feel good and he was definitely feeling her.

I felt a soft touch on my back and it sent a chill down my spine. It was Riccy; she looked at me as if someone had just died. She whispered in my ear, "I'm sorry, baby, but you needed to see this for yourself. He's still fucking her."

I couldn't take it a minute longer my blood was boiling. I refuse to be looking like a fool for anyone. I turned around and said, "This was some sort of set up? What the hell were you trying to do? Humiliate me, Riccy?!" My ears were ringing like I was in a fire house. *Toi calm down* are the words I was hearing. A sense of calmness took over and I walked towards the pool table. Remember no matter how bad your heart is breaking never let a nigga bring you to the point of becoming street trash. Ms. Toi will always be a lady. But it was becoming a struggle.

D didn't see me until I reached the edge of the table. But Desiree certainly did and was giving me an eye full. He was leaning up against the table with his hand placed on the small of her back and she was whispering in his ear. I approached with the elegance of a queen.

"Excuse me I hope I'm not interrupting you two." D turned around and looked at me with a blank stare. He removed his hand as though she had become a contagious disease.

"Damn Toi when did you get back?"

I noticed a few people looking around for a show, but best believe they wouldn't be getting one from me. Who the hell do I look like? -- Rent a movie or watch Ricky Lake if need some damn entertainment. The IDs were in my hand. I released them on the pool table and walked away. Before I could even get to the exit, D was on my heels.

"Toi come here!" The sound of his voice made me ill to my stomach. He caught up quick and grabbed me by the arm. "You hear me talking to you?" He said like he had a reason to be pissed. Next thing I knew we were in the parking lot and he had a kung fu grip on my arm. I pulled my arm away as we approached his car. I felt him come from behind and slam me. He looked at me with fear in his eyes and said, "Toi what you trying to do, leave me now!? Yo' ass ain't going nowhere!"

My eyes were burning like they were on fire as the tears flowed down my face. My voice trembled as words escaped my lips, "How could you look at me the other night and tell me you loved me? D, I haven't even been gone for 24 hours and this is how you are carrying me!?

This game you want to play with my life, I can't be a part of anymore! You have no respect for me at all. And you have the nerve to carry your shit in public like this!?"

His face held no expression when he said, "Get in the car!" I know he must have lost his mind if he thought I was going anywhere with him tonight. He was so close to my face I could smell the liquor draining from his mouth. "Please don't have me hurt you out here Toi." Fear should have probably taken over my body but the anger I was feeling was much stronger. At this point D was nothing but a liar in my eyes. All the hurt I was feeling came out beyond my control as I pushed him back. Obviously he was shocked because it took him a moment before he went completely crazy.

My world froze for a moment.

D pulled my head back and looked into my eyes as though he had become possessed. "Girl you better not ever think about laying your hands on me again! You have the nerve to ask me if I love you? Better believe if another bitch ever touched me their ass would be meeting their maker right now!" Finally he let me go and pushed me into the car.

My body felt numb and cold as though I was having an out of body experience. This man had my heart in the worst way and the more I reflect on it the angrier I become with myself. *Lawd why am I allowing him to treat me this way?* I hate losing control like this. Those three little words keep ringing in my ear, "I LOVE YOU". It amazes me the power of those words. They make you feel on top of the world one moment and like you're in hell the next.

I began to count the lights in the street as my vision became a blur. Before I realized it we were in front of his house.

"Come on get out."

My body was limp like all the energy I possessed had been drained. D opened the door and pulled me up. His home no longer brought me the peace it once upon a time had. Now it felt like a prison. As I sank my feet into his plush carpet I started having vague memories of my daddy. Me lying on his chest and falling asleep to the rhythm of his beat. I felt like I had come upon a theory. Maybe this is what I have been in search of, the unconditional love that my daddy once provided me with.

D interrupted my thoughts with his weak voice, "Toi, come here." I needed his words of comfort like a dying soul searching for their last breath. My body wanted to come to him, but my legs wouldn't move. He caressed my shoulder and asked me to look at him. "Baby believe me when I say this because it's from my heart. We are never going to go through this again. Ain't no bitch on this earth worth me losing you over!"

Words… so many words I thought. So many promises never kept. I no longer was breaking down. D had broken me down the moment I laid my eyes on him. The warnings had always been clear, but I chose to ignore the obvious. It didn't matter now-- too much time had passed and it was too late to turn back. And to be truthful I didn't want to.

The tears that fell on D's chest that night could have filled the driest river. Betrayal is the worst feeling in the world. And it seemed as though I had been experiencing a lot of that lately. Everyone in my life seemed to be disappointing me. Chanelle, D and now Sharice. Momma has allowed a man to come between us. Part of D's heart wants another woman, and Riccy, set me up. My heart believes her intentions were genuine, but the betrayal is still present.

His soft kisses brushed across my forehead as I lay there searching for a sense of peace. "Toi you sleep?"

I cleared my raspy voice and said no. He adjusted our bodies in another position and then began to speak again. However, now D's voice was back in control. The urgency was no longer there. "You keep talking about how your mom's has been tripping, why you don't just move in with me?" He sat there waiting on my response as I thought about his request.

"Move in with you? Where is this coming from?"

D started laughing and said, "That's not the response I thought I was going to get." The laughter had faded away and his aggravation was becoming apparent, "Toi don't play with me just answer the question." The words he wanted to hear I could not provide right now.

"Baby can we talk about this later? I want to go home." D began to pace the room and then finally sat down on the couch.

His breathing started to become labored and it was making me uneasy. "Toi, you want to go home? I just asked your ass to move in with me and all you can say is that you want to go home. What the fuck is that about?!"

This conversation was definitely being blown all out of proportion. And I certainly wasn't feeling his mood or tone. This entire evening had been a disaster. Now he had the nerve to get an attitude because I won't bow down to his request. My spirit was weak and I knew I needed to get home .The guilt and fear of me leaving had him acting like this. I swear it's killing me, but his ass is going to have to suffer. Let him feel the pain I was feeling!

"D, baby I am not trying to argue with you tonight. Just take me home. I know Sharice is having a fit about now." D grabbed his jacket and walked towards the door. As I proceeded to follow him he turned around and grabbed me by the throat. My ear felt as though hot lava was pouring down my lobes.

"You fucked that nigga while you were gone, didn't you? That's why you talking all that shit tonight!" I tried to pull away so I could make a connection with his eyes but his grip was to strong. His words continued to burn my ears.

"Your ass always complaining about Sharice and your Momma.What about me? I'm fucking laid up in this house with you, when I should be out getting shit handled! Messing around with you is fucking up my flow. My ass needs to be focused on some other shit, besides your whining ass!"

My heart dropped with every word that poured out of his mouth. I couldn't believe he was talking to me like this.

I decided it would be in my best interest to keep my mouth shut. Shit was tense between us and I just couldn't handle much more.

The pressure of his grip began to release as he sat slowly on the coach. His words sent the worst surge of energy through my veins. The man who just was standing upon me like a strong soldier had now fallen. He held his head and began to rock back and forth.

"Baby, talk to me, what's wrong?" D's rocking had stopped and he sat there as though he had become deaf and mute. I occupied the space beside him and began to rub his back. "D, please say something, look at me. Tell me what's wrong."

Cursed by the Candy

The only response that escaped his body was him shaking his head left to right. My tears hit the floor as I placed myself in front of him and tried to look at the expression that had consumed his face. My body froze in horror when I saw his eyes. The whites of his eyes now only held the color of blood. The pain and fear I saw upon his face will haunt me forever.

I began to panic and D just sat there as if nothing was happening. I just barely heard the words coming from his mouth, "Toi, baby just calm down. Go in the kitchen and just get me some Tylenol and something to drink."

I looked at him as though he had lost his mind. "Tylenol? D what in world is Tylenol going to do?! My voice became elevated and I said, "We need to go the hospital!" My strong king just sat there with tears rolling down his face as he gathered enough strength to just lie back on the couch. I knew I wasn't helping matters at all by being hysterical, so I just fulfilled his request for the medicine.

I would have to face the wrath of Chanelle later. There was no way I was leaving D tonight.

When I returned back into the room, D was fast asleep or so I prayed. I sat down beside him and caressed his moist tear streaking skin. His weak eyes opened in response to my touch.

"Baby let me get you into the bed."

As I struggled to get him into the bed, the vibe I was feeling from him scared me to the bone. I'm hardly a doctor, but I knew something was terribly wrong. D slept all night and most of the next day. I felt helpless as I laid beside his body and prayed.

"God, please take this pain away."

At that moment there was no doubt in my mind that I would be moving in with him. I just needed to gather enough strength to tell Chanelle.

Chapter 6

The longer I lay there the more uncomfortable I had become. I tried to carefully place D in another position so I could sleep. I curled my body into his and began to smell the strong scent of his cologne in the pillow. The smell that normally calmed me was now making me ill. A hot and watery taste took over my mouth and the urge to vomit was undeniable. I rushed into the bathroom and gripped the toilet.

My head was spinning as the urine escaped from my bladder and the vomit rushed from my mouth.

All of the commotion had awakened D. I heard slow footsteps behind me. "Toi, damn girl what's wrong?" I tried to speak but another round of vomit had escaped my mouth. D handed me a warm washcloth and sat down on the side of the tub. His words took me by surprise, but really I don't know why-- it's not like me a D had been practicing safe sex at all. "Toi, yo' ass pregnant?"

Pregnant... that definitely had never even crossed my mind until now. But now the more I think about it I had definitely been feeling sick lately. I wiped my face with the warm rag and then began to speak, "Baby I don't think so."

I asked him how he was feeling and he started laughing and said, "Better than you. Shit and I'm glad the way you jumped up. If my head had still been hurting, I would have been messed up for real.

I just smiled and said sorry. I thought to myself, *Thank you God for answering my prayers.* My stomach was feeling better so I tried to pull myself up. D grabbed my arm and said, "Come here." We sat on the side of the tub and looked at each other for a minute without words.

Finally D broke the silence and said, "Toi, I'm sorry." Those words meant the world to me. I feel like it takes a real man to admit when he's wrong. My head found a home on his shoulder as he placed a soft kiss upon my crown. I was hoping that this was a truce between us. All of the arguing we had been doing lately had really become draining.

The next day I was experiencing the same urge and I immediately knew I was probably pregnant. D was in the kitchen handling his business when I approached him with the news, "Baby I am going to get a pregnancy test today." He pushed the scale over and said in a nonchalant manner, "For real." I was taken back by his response and a bit irritated. You would have thought I said I was going to the mall.

"That's all you have to say?"

D turned around and said, "Damn Toi what you want me to say? If you're pregnant, you having my baby. Ain't shit else to discuss." Every day that I spend with this man is a learning experience. Daily a different personality appears.

"Oh I see you have this all figured out!? So what am I supposed to do? Drop out of school and live off your ass for the rest of my life?"

D rotated his neck around as if he was stretching and said, "Look this is exactly what I am talking about. You see me sitting here trying to take care of something and you keep talking! Baby just calm down. I am about to take you home so you can pack your shit." He touched my face and said, "Let me handle this and everything will be straight."

~~~~~

The second I stepped into the house-- all hell broke loss and I was bombarded with questions. Mike in my face,

Chanelle in my ear and Mr. Charles, who had become a fixture in our house, sitting back like this was a movie or something. Chanelle was in rare form today and I couldn't get a feel on the direction she was about to take.

"Toi I guess all of the talking I have been doing lately has not meant a damn thing! Sit your black ass down and carefully listen to every word I'm about to say to you! Never in my life have I ever been so disappointed. Tell me what the hell did I do wrong?!"

I tried to focus on a spot in the corner so I could drown Chanelle out, but it didn't work. Her words had overpowered my thought process. I had already tried to prepare myself for the drama, but nothing could have prepared me for this. I focused on my poor brother sitting in the chair. He looked just as helpless as me. I searched his face for guidance but he just turned around.

"Toi this is it! Momma can't take it anymore. I have been sitting here sick with worry for the last two days. Sharice said your little drug boy dragged you out of the club. I'm thinking you are under a rock dead or something. Toi, why are you doing this?" I started focusing on my anger instead of Chanelle's words. Now Riccy is telling my business? Shit, did she tell anyone that she set me up to look like a sucker!? All of this drama could be immediately ended if I told Chanelle I was pregnant, but I decided to allow her to vent.

"Toi, what are you doing? When is the last time you went to school? And don't even try and fix your mouth to lie, the school has been calling here every time your ass skips! Is the nigga that important?"

I just stared down at the floor. Chanelle leaned down and said, "Look at me when I am speaking to you!" I raised my head and stared in her face as the tears expressed the pain I was feeling. Mike finally had enough.

He stood up and said, "Let me talk to her, Ma." Chanelle took his advice and went back to her company. I don't know who she thinks she is fooling, that's all she wanted to do anyway.

Mike took a seat next to me and sighed as he ran his fingers over his waves. "Girl what's going on?" The concern in his voice made this even more difficult.

I couldn't hold it back another minute I just blurted out, "Mike… I'm pregnant!" It seemed like a million years before he responded, but when he finally did I swear I felt the walls tremor.

"PREGNANT?! Toi have you lost your damn mind?! Who in the hell are you pregnant by?" I looked at him and felt disgusted. How could he even ask me something like that?! His fatherly tone was about to drive me crazy. "Toi ,what are you doing? Yo' ass has come down to VA and lost focus of everything. What happened to the girl with attitude and self esteem so high it even got on my nerves?"

Every word that left his mouth cut like a knife. He was right, Ms. Toi was gone now and I didn't know how to get her back. A mixture of emotions had taken over my body and I began to feel aggravated with Mike.

"Damn since when have you become so perfect? Was I judgmental when you were having your little problem? No, I always stood beside you. So don't sit here in my face with this holier than thou attitude, because I don't want to hear it! I come to you for support and encouragement and this is how you treat me!?"

Mike started laughing which really threw me off. "Toi you're real funny. I don't give a damn about your feelings right now. I care about your life and how you are trying to fuck it up. Since when have you started letting a nigga control you like this? And a baby-- you know Chanelle is going to have a fit."

I couldn't take it another minute. "Mike it doesn't matter anyway because I am about to move in with D."

The look on my brother's face undeniably sent chills through me. I had never seen him so mad before. "No you're not! I will hurt that brotha first. Toi, you think I'm playing, walk up out of this house with D!" I swear I didn't know whether to take him seriously or not. I had never seen him take on this gangsta role.

"Mike, please let me do this. I need you to be there for me and the baby. Please don't turn your back on me." My tired body just lay on the coach and I cried my daily flood of tears. Mike just sat there and stared at me in silence and then kissed me on the forehead.

He moved slowly towards the door before he stopped and said, "Toi don't be a fool."

I wanted to get up and pack, but everyone's word had drained my soul. I looked over at my family's pictures and thought about the simpler times when everyone was happy and seemed to be on the same track. But who am I fooling, those are only distant memories now.

Toi what are you doing? The demons that reside in my mind were speaking to me again. *Chanelle won't even miss you. But D needs you and right now you need him more.*

The trance that had consumed my body was broken when I heard the door slam. I managed to look out the window when I saw Chanelle pulling out of the driveway. I guess in a way I was relieved but part of me was hurt she let it go that easily.

~~~~~

Sleep has become my existence the last couple of days. My frame feels exhausted and strained. Vomiting every hour is certainly not helping. I had to find some kind of peace with Chanelle-- I decided to write her a letter.

Dear Chanelle,

I am so sorry that I have become such a disappointment to you. Words can't begin to express how lonely I have been since we have moved here. You have a different life now momma. And I no longer feel the bond that we once had. What I am going to tell you will no doubt break your heart. But I have to live my life now. Chanelle, I am pregnant, and you have expressed your feelings about this subject to me all my life so I'm trying to make this as painless as I can for everyone, especially you. I will be moving out tonight because I cannot bear to see the disappointment in your eyes another day. Momma my wings have become restless under your roof and now I have to find my own way .I'll be in touch.

Love Toi,

P.S - Tell Mike thank you and I love him.

Regret pain and sorrow smeared the ink on my paper. I felt so sick and alone. Yes I had D, but family is the core of your soul.

I couldn't believe how so many things had changed in a matter of months. Depression was waving its ugly hand and I no longer had the strength to fight it.

As I tried to get my belongings together Mike called from downstairs, "Toi, Sharice is coming up." I continued to keep myself busy so I wouldn't have to look at her. My family had betrayed me, and for that she was like a stranger on the street to me. My whole life Sharice had represented peace and happiness to me. She was my only real confidante. We were more like sisters than cousins.

The moment she stepped over the threshold the tension became apparent.

She entered the room trying to get a since of the vibe I was sending off.

"Hey, what's going on?" Her presence felt like a parasite that had invaded my body. My hands began to sweat and my heart took on a beat of anger.

"Are you kidding me Sharice?! What are you doing here, are you trying to teach me another lesson? If that's the case no thank you. Your little session called school for suckers ended the other night. So pretty much anything you have to say to me I don't want to hear!"

Sharice looked at me as though she was shocked. She began to approach me, but the evil glare that had consumed my face stopped her.

"Toi, don't act like this girl, I was just trying to look out for you, not hurt you. You know I would never do anything like that.

As I looked up from my dresser and saw my reflection in the mirror, the truth hit me. I knew she had good intentions but at this point it was the principle. I positioned myself so I could look directly at her, "Sharice you have been my best friend since we were five. There were so many other ways you could have approached this situation. My faith and trust in you has been damaged and I don't know if we will be able to repair that." The hurt in Sharice's eyes made my heart drop, but my pride wouldn't allow me to give in.

She stood up and said, "Toi, you're my family and I hope you find it in your heart one day to just let this be. A man should never come between families. Remember your own words, you said them to me not so long ago in regards to Chanelle… take your own advice." Sharice grabbed her purse and started to leave. She stopped at the door and said,

"I will be leaving in August, I got accepted to Spellman. Emotions captured the structure of my face and the tears began to fall. Not because I was sad, but because this has been her dream and I knew how important this was for her. I surrendered my pride and embraced her.

"Girl I am so proud of you."

Those were the only words I could manage to say. But honestly no other words were necessary. Sharice knew my heart almost as much as I did. I tried to block out the common sense that I knew I still possessed. The direction of my life had become so unfamiliar to me. How could I even be allowing myself to go through all this drama? I sat their straining for answers my heart no longer provided. The image I saw was no longer Toi. The young girl with hopes and dreams and positive energy had now been replaced with greed, selfishness and a sense of insecurity. The thought of me actually bringing someone into the world was terrifying. How could I be so stupid?! A child needs a stable environment. Not a hustler's life.

D could be shot, go to jail, anything. My breathing started to become erratic and I knew I had to calm down. So I did the only thing I knew to do... I prayed.

Lawd, please forgive my sins. Guide me in the right direction. My soul has become lost. My child needs a fair chance at this world. Please help me. In Jesus name I say, Amen...

As I was kneeling down on my bed I felt a warm comforting presence from behind. I got up to see who it was and D was standing in my doorway. "Baby how long have you been their?"He kissed me softly on the lips and said, "Long enough." He started inspecting the room and then said, "Are you ready to go?"

I placed my hands around his neck and said, "Baby I'm trying but I just don't have the energy." He looks down at me with the most beautiful smile and I realize this is why I love this man the way I do.

"Toi forget this stuff. Leave it. Baby whatever you need I'll get it. I'm your provider now. You don't have to worry about anything. You hear me?"

I inhaled his scent and thought *my warrior always had the right words.* He peered into my eyes with this heartfelt expression. "Toi, the hard part has already been accomplished. You already have my heart, now you're carrying me seed. Baby, respect our privacy and relationship and everything else will fall in place."

Chapter 7

The last three months have flown right by. I would have never imagined living with D would bring me so much joy. My baby is definitely a man of his word. Our home is a place of tranquility. No chick coming around or calling and his business is booming out of control. He tells me every day that I am his good luck charm.

And of course money is never an issue. I have at least 5 G's accessible at all times. But ladies every fairytale has its down side. Being pregnant is no joke. My emotions are all over the place. One minute I'm happy the next I'm crying. But D takes everything day by day with me and for that I am genuinely grateful.

The majority of the time I am alone, but that's ok because I do realize that is part of the game. He definitely cannot make the paper if he is sitting up under me all the time. But one thing I must say is my baby shows respect. Always in the house by 1:30 or 2 and he checks in all day long.

He knows there are no ifs, ands or buts about coming to the doctor with me to all appointments. This child is ours so his presence is always required. So business sometimes has to be put on the back burner whenever I have an appointment. However, I'm going to make an exception when I find out the sex. I want that to be a special surprise.

I am hoping it is a boy. He never says he wants a boy, but what man doesn't want a young man around that represents himself.

These days my number one priority is my family. I'm sad to say that I had to drop out of school because it had become a distraction. However I am working on getting my GED. Ms. Toi will have some form of paper to show she has an education. Even if it is just my GED.

I hear the familiar sound of keys and I instantly get excited. The moment he enters the house he grabs me tight and talks to our child. Ladies throughout your life I hope you one day experience this kind of love. He lifts me carefully and places me on the kitchen counter. I look down at his smooth chocolate skin and say, "I see you missed us today?"

My words are soft as I place kisses on his neck. The scent of his cologne sends chills down my spin.

He puts me back on the ground and then says, "Can't you tell? Damn baby if money didn't motivate me the way it does I would never leave this house. That's why shit is popping off the way it is because I'm trying to provide the glamorous life for you and my baby."

I gaze into his eyes and say, "Baby without you there is no life for me and our child. Please be careful . . . Promise us that!"

D finally speaks after a moment and his words are deep. "Toi no other person has ever made me feel so wanted. Please listen to what I am saying to you carefully. My momma and daddy loved me. But I never have felt love like this. I appreciate everything you do for me. Your heart is selfless when it comes to us. You seem to find enjoyment in the taking care of me. You put me before yourself and that's real love.

Toi I deal with shady ass people every day, but when I step through those doors all that shit is forgotten. I just want you to know I cherish what we have, and this gift that you're about to give me.

I'm about to wrap this up but just one more thing… All of this money doesn't mean shit without you. Word is bond."

D went into the bathroom and I sat down on the sofa trying to digest his words. I realize that it takes a lot for any man to express his feelings. But for a hustler it is unheard of. They see it as a sign of weakness. Everyone is an enemy to them. Letting your guard down for a minute could be the end of your existence.

D returned back into the room and lay in my arms. No words were really required, but I felt a need just to say, "Thank you."

He pulled away from my embrace and said, "Toi come outside with me." I tried to pull him back down but he objected.

"Baby why? Is everything okay?"

D stood up and said, "Stop asking so many questions and come on."

I put on my slippers and followed him outside. The instant we turned the corner I laid my eyes on the most beautiful black and silver Land Cruiser. My baby is a show off so you know it had to be equipped with a big silver bow on the roof.

I walked over to the truck and covered my mouth to contain my scream. "Baby I know you didn't buy me a truck?!?" D just smiled and stood they're all proud. I could no longer control my excitement and I started jumping up and down and ran over to the track.

D's smile disappeared and he said, "Toi, calm your ass down before you mess around and lose my baby!" I ignored his concern and jumped into this fabulous piece of machinery, put the keys in the ignition and it purred like a kitten. I swear this was too good to be true.

I glanced over and noticed an envelope in the seat. I thought, *What in the world could this possibly be?*

A puzzled expression came over my face "Baby what is this?"

He said, "Just open it, Toi." When I opened it up I still had questions. The envelope contained a small key that was around a gold chain.

"D I still don't know what this is."

He grabbed my chin and said, "Toi nobody is promised a day. Baby this life I live isn't forever. It's the law of the game. I will either end up dead or in jail eventually. And I want to make sure you and baby are provided for. If anything ever happens to me I want you to use this key. It's to a safety deposit box. I have put 75 G's in there for you as of today. And will continue to put money in there for our future. Baby no matter what, never tell anyone about this.

His words paralyzed the essence of my soul. "D stop talking like that! You better not ever leave us!"

D held me tight and said, "I'll try not to ...Go put some clothes on and lets go for a ride."

That night the vultures were out in full effect. Since I had started showing I definitely limited my outside activity. Of course I had the occasional shopping spree; that was definitely a requirement to keep my sanity. Plus I had to stay sexy for my baby. Remember pregnant or not always stay on top of your game or your man will most certainly be lusting in another direction. But I must say the whole club scene had come to an abrupt stop after the incident with Desiree.

D said he had to make a run to Magic's real quick and asked me to come .This took me by surprise because Magic's was for old heads this particular night. We pulled up and I noticed the cars were different. Not the bling that normally occupied the lot, but regular cars like these people had 9-5's.

"Come on get out." I did what I was instructed to do .The moment I walked into the club I felt queasy .The room was full of smoke. And old heads were wall to wall. Playing dominoes, cards and talking loud as hell.

D grabbed my hand and lead me over towards this table .The moment I looked into her eyes I knew this had to be D's mother. She was about 5'5 with a dark mahogany complexion. She appeared to be tired as though this world had dealt her a raw deal. D approached her with love and said, "Hey ma how are you doing?"

Cursed by the Candy

She looked at him and said, "I'm ok what about yourself?" In the middle of her sentence she finally notices my presence. Instantly I feel like an intruder under her judgmental eyes. "Don Don who is this?"

D held my hand and said, "Ma this is Toi."

His mother offers no sign of affection. In a cold tone she says, "Hello, what are you one of my sons gold digging hoes?"

I couldn't believe what I was hearing. It took everything I had not to cuss this woman out.

D immediately interrupted her outburst, "What the hell is wrong with you talking to her like that?! This is the woman carrying your grandchild. Show some respect. Ma, apologize to her now or this will be the last time you get any money from me. I hate to disrespect you, but the only gold digger I see in here is you."

I realized that D was mad, but I couldn't sit here and listen to him talk to his mother like that. Even though she deserved it.

I tugged on his shirt and said, "Baby that's enough, I'm ok. Let's just go." D seemed to be ignoring my plea so I turned around and started towards the door. I couldn't wait to get out of here, the smoke was starting to become unbearable.

Cursed by the Candy

D finally noticed I was gone as I approached the exit sign. "Toi wait baby you don't have to leave." His words were comforting but I knew I had to diffuse the situation. I looked over in his mother's direction and said, "It was nice meeting you." And I walked out.

D followed my lead as his mother trailed behind. Then I heard his words from a distance, "Ma this is why I love and respect her, because she always carries herself like a lady."

I held my head up high as I made my way to the car. But the moment I stepped in, the emotions took over and the tears began to fall. This playing my position shit is taking a toll on me, but only for love of this man will I belittle myself....

The encounter with D's mother had me reflecting on my own relationship with Chanelle. It had been almost three months since I last spoke to her. Chanelle pisses me off no doubt, but I know she only has the best intentions for me. The holidays were approaching and I really was starting to miss my family.

Mike and I hang out sometimes, but things are definitely not the same.

D got in the car and it was as if the incident with his mother never happened. We left the club that evening and never spoke about it again. Now you know I wanted to, but I saw how upset he was and I definitely didn't want to stir up any bad memories.

~~~~~

My mind was going crazy trying to figure out what to get D for Christmas. What in the world do you get for someone who has everything? And then a lightbulb went off in my brain .This idea was so exciting I couldn't wait.

This was the week I found out the sex of our child. I didn't tell D about it yet so this would be perfect. I decided to have the ultrasound picture blown up and framed. And in gold letters girl or boy. I knew this would be appreciated more than anything I could purchase at a store.

I couldn't believe how nervous I was sitting in the doctor's office. My heart wanted a healthy baby, but my soul wanted boy. I closed my eyes tight and prayed for a healthy baby son.

Thoughts began to invade my mind. *How could I guide a girl when I was so lost myself?*

Seconds later the doctor called me back. As I traveled down the hall a familiar voice caught my attention. I almost broke my neck trying to see who it was. As I turned the corner the familiar voice became a reality. It was Marquetta and that same brotha I saw beat her down that night. I began to wonder if she was in here for the same reason I was. As I made my way down the long corridor our shoulders brushed as we passed by like strangers.

This was a perfect example of a silly bitch. She's angry with me for not helping her that evening and the more I think about it the happier I am that I didn't. Her ass is still dealing with him. But for real who am I to judge anyone?

I placed my body on the white paper and slid back my clothing. The cold jelly solution made me jump as he ran the instrument across my child. His voice sounded like the angel that had answered my prayers.

"Well, Toi it looks like you are having a baby boy." I was so happy I almost jumped off of the table. Me thinking about the expression on D's face made my heart skip a beat .The moment I stepped into the house visions of our son took over my mind.

The doorbell rang and almost scared me to death .Who could that possibly be? No one ever comes over when D's not home. I cautiously looked out of the peephole and was shocked to see Desiree standing there.

I slowly opened the door and looked at her as though she had lost all of her senses. I couldn't believe this bitch had the nerve to come over here. Company was the last thing in the world I was expecting today. However the house was in tip top condition like always. And my appearance was above average. Must stay fly for my baby at all times.

I took a deep breath and then said, "What are you doing here? I know damn well D didn't invite you!" Desiree held this arrogant expression on her face which caused me to feel uneasy for a moment.

She smiled and said "I'm not here to see D, I'm here to see you!"

Curiosity was starting to get the best of me so I wished she would just come out with it. I motioned for her to come in then I stood next to the door. I had to get myself together and quick .This chick was not going to come into my house and run shit. I noticed her looking around observing our decor and more than likely hating every minute of it. We had professional pictures of us over the fireplace outlined with various trips we had been on. You would have had to be blind not to notice them.

In a moment Ms.Toi's representative was about to surface-- now don't get it twisted I am a Diva on any day. But my representative takes it to another level no doubt.

I knew this chick expected me to get all ghetto, but I was about to flip that on her. Remember kill 'em with kindness.

I turned around and greeted her with a smile then said, "So, Ms. Desiree how can I help you?" I knew I had caught her off guard because she sat there looking at me as though I was crazy. Then I noticed her staring at my stomach.

Cursed by the Candy

She looked at her watch then said, "Oh I heard you were pregnant."

I was about to let her finish but I couldn't resist, "Yeah me and D are expecting." The jealousy was written all over her face and I was loving it. Now Desiree is about as red as they come without being white so right now she was as red as a beet.

I looked over at the clock because for real this was starting to get boring. She needed to state her business and get out.

"So what do you want to talk about?"

Desiree made herself comfortable on my coach which pissed me off. She crossed her legs and smiled. Then the words that escaped her mouth will dwell in my memory forever.

"Oh I guess we are going to have to learn to get along since our children will be related." My eyes became so small I could barely see. My mouth dropped but from the inside. This chick will never get a reaction out of me. I rubbed my belly and then said, "Will you excuse me for a moment?"

I went into the kitchen and grabbed two glasses of milk. When I returned to the living room Desiree was hating on our pictures.

I stood beside her and said, "I hate to interrupt you, but since both of us are expecting it's important that we stay healthy." I handed her the milk and motioned for her to have a seat.

Ladies take notes. Never do the obvious. Emotions can mess up everything. I refused to let this chick have the upper hand on me. My insides were melting away but I had to keep up the charade.

Desiree placed the milk on the table as if I had tried to poison her. Next thing I knew she was heading towards the door. I stood up and said, "You're leaving so soon? Don't you want to finish talking? Better yet why don't you wait till D comes home and break the news to him?"

She stopped and said, "Stupid, everyone already knows except you! D keeps you in here like a slave while he's out doing his thing! He really got you thinking you a fucking princess!"

She smiled and said, "Don't get too comfortable." Her smile sent cold sweat down the back of my neck .The door slammed and the cold air flew across my face.

My body was paralyzed from her words. I ran to the bathroom just in time for the vomit to escape my mouth. As I sat on the cold tile I wished there was someone I could talk to. These days it just seemed like it's me, myself and I. I never thought about being in here like a slave. But the more I thought about her words the more apparent it became. I was definitely an outsider. D's princess he kept in his own world.

I rubbed my stomach and begged God for his help."Please Lord tell me this isn't true…" D and this baby are my life and the thought of me sharing him is unbearable.

My tears had become a ritual. Someday I knew they would no longer fall and that's when the pain would start to deteriorate my insides.

I had to stay busy because if I didn't I would just go crazy. My baby definitely didn't need to feel the stress I was feeling. And I knew he did.

The Christmas tree I had in the corner caught my attention so I decided to put it together. This was supposed to be an enjoyable event, but the sorrow I was feeling didn't allow me to enjoy anything.

When I finished I walked near the window seat and peered into the parking lot .The personalized ornaments were sitting on the floor gathering dust .Who would have imagined that just a few hours ago I was on cloud nine? Today was supposed to be special. Our first tree and the surprise of our baby boy...

I sat there for hours and watched the snow gather in the parking lot. That's when I noticed D pulling up. Knots began to form in my stomach. *Lawd please calm me down, if only for my child.*

A few minutes later D walked into the dark Christmas lit house. He walked around the room for a few before he noticed me sitting in the dark.

"Damn, Toi you scared a nigga! What are you doing sitting in the dark?"

I sat in the window with my knees to my chest. He walked over and placed a kiss on my cheek. I didn't have the energy to beat around the bush; I just let him have it.

"I had a visitor today!"

A curious expression consumed his face, "Ok, who was it?"

A lump began to form in my throat as I attempted to speak. And then my pain began to drop on the pillow. D touched my knee and said, "What the hell is going on Toi!"

His touch infuriated me. "D, no, you tell me what is going on! Desiree came over here today and informed me that you have another child on the way! When were you going to tell me?"

The next thing I knew D had stood up and grabbed his keys off of the counter and walked out the door. I looked out the window and watched him skid out of the parking lot. I didn't know what to do so I grabbed the phone to call him. After about five rings he picked up the phone.

"D what are you doing and where are you going?"

D just said, "Baby we'll talk when I get back. I need to do something real quick." The next thing I heard was the dial tone.

~~~~~

An hour later D was standing in the living room with Desiree. He pushed her through the door and said, "Tell her the truth and now!"

Desiree's eye was black and purple and her hair was all over the place. I couldn't believe what I was witnessing. Desiree stood before me and cried like a baby.

Before I knew what happened D pulled her head back and placed a gun to her temple and said, "You had so much to say earlier spit that shit out now!"

She tried to mumble a few words but I couldn't understand what she was saying.

I looked at D and pleaded with him to stop with my eyes. Finally Desiree admitted she was lying. My body held no emotion at the time. I looked at her helpless body and wondered if she knew her lie could have cost her life?

D definitely had me on edge and it scared me to death. To think he would do something this dramatic to prove a point. How could I even know if she was lying or not? Given the circumstances she would say anything.

Cursed by the Candy

D put the gun away and told Desiree to get out. She stood up and almost fell back down as she struggled to exit our home.

It amazes me how I actually had the urge to help this girl who tried to destroy my life. But I guess that's just the human in us all.

I watched D just stand there consumed with hate. This was the first time I can ever say I was genuinely afraid of him.

His silhouette in the corner had my nerves on edge. I tried to comfort the goose bumps forming on my arms but nothing seemed to help.

D began to approach me like a shadow in the night. My legs wanted to move but my body wouldn't cooperate.

D bent down on his knees and placed his arms around my waist. Then I felt his rain began to saturate my shirt.

He slowly began to remove my shirt and placed gentle kisses on our child. I looked down at his head and thought to myself, this is all Desiree wanted. Unconditional love....

I began to caress the back of his head as he spoke to our son. I no longer could keep my secret.

I said, "I hope you show this kind of love to our son when he gets here."

D let go of my stomach and stood up. "Don't play with me Toi. You're giving me a son?"

I just smiled and shook my head yes.

D walked over to the tree and gazed into the lights. Finally he spoke, "Baby you know this is the first tree I've had since I was ten, my momma started drugs then. She never thought about Christmas, the only thing that was on her mind was that glass dick." His words held all the hurt and pain of his past. At that moment I fully understood his action towards Desiree. His fear of losing us as a family had taken him to another place.

D sat back down beside me and said, "Baby I can't believe the Lord has blessed me with you and now a son. I have done so many things in my past I'm just scared that they are going to come back and haunt me one day.

Sometimes I watch you sleep and wonder what in the world have I done to deserve you. Toi you are my guardian angel.

Baby I hate to treat you like a prisoner, but I need you to lay low for a while. Please don't leave out unless we're together. I have a lot of enemies that would love to get their hands on you just to hurt me. Niggas know you are the only thing that really matters. Plus I think we need to move up out of here and soon.

Everything D was saying I had already been thinking about. I am hardly naive to this world. I knew the moment word got out that I was carrying D's baby I became an asset to his rivals. Him telling me to stay in the house was not as traumatic as he thought it would be. As long as we were safe and together everything was ok with me.

D lay in my lap and we talked all night.

"Baby I am going to start looking for somewhere to move this week. I wanna be outta here by Christmas.

I looked down at him and said, "So soon?"

He stretched and said, "I don't see any reason to prolong it. We gotta get the hell outta here."

His urgency made me a bit nervous I must admit .Was there something going on I didn't know about? One thing I don't do is get into my man's business, but something this evening made me want to ask, "D is everything ok? Are you sure there's nothing you want to tell me?"

D just rubbed my face and said, "Trust me baby, everything is good."

One thing I know about D is when his mind is set on something it is only a matter of time before it becomes a reality.

Cursed by the Candy

Two weeks later you better believe we were moving into a five-bedroom house on a lake.

Chapter 8

My baby was extravagant so anything he put his energy into was big.

And this was certainly the case with our new home. When we pulled into the complex I could hardly believe my eyes. This house was huge and had D written all over it.

I stared at our home in amazement, when D broke me out of my trance.

"Toi, you going to sit here all day or come in?"

I turned around and kissed D on the cheek and said, "Come on let's go."

D opened the door as I stood there thinking I can't believe he pulled this off so quickly.

The moment I walked through the door this place felt like home.

It had an aura to it that was unmistakable. I laid my feet into the carpet and could not believe this was real. I felt like I was floating on a cloud. The cathedral ceilings made the house appear to be massive. And to top it off the entire ceiling was made of glass.

As I walked into the living room and admired the sky all I could think about were little diamonds. I believe this had to be the clearest night I had ever witnessed.

It was more then apparent that D had everything pre-arranged. In the corner of the living room set a 15-foot Christmas tree. For a moment I thought we were in Rockefeller Plaza.

I walked over to the tree and noticed the personalized ornaments I had made. In a flash my emotions took over and the tears began to fall. D had another one made and it said Little Donte. What was even more unique is that it had the baby's ultra sound picture on it.

D kissed my neck softly and said, "We are not going to have the water works tonight Toi. Stop crying this is suppose to be a happy time." He turned me around and placed a scarf around my eyes and said, "Come here. It felt like I was in the dark forever, but when the light appeared again I couldn't believe my eyes.

I went into the room and rubbed my hands across the railing of the crib. What my baby had done was amazing. The entire room was blue and the walls were blessed with the name "Little D".

This was unmistakably a child's paradise. There was every sports figure you could imagine accented through the room. There was no doubt in my mind that our child would be spoiled.

I was so overwhelmed with excitement I felt dizzy. I found a home in this blue and white rocking chair. I couldn't help but to imagine that the baby was in my arms. It felt so real as though I could feel his small frame.

D came over to me and said, "Baby are you ok?"

I just smiled at my strong soldier and said, "I'm more than ok." My feet found support within the carpet as I wrapped my arms around his neck. "Baby words can't explain how grateful I am for you. Thank you so much."

He looked into my eyes and said, "Toi thank you, for giving me a life and a reason to live."

The vibration of his pager interrupted our intimate moment. I looked at the mirror in the corner and could see the silhouette of D's face. He stared at the pager and a glare of concern penetrated his face. I slid to the end of the rocking chair and cleared my throat. "Baby, help me up please," D placed the pager in his pocket and knelt down in front of the chair. He pushed my hair from my eyes and placed his wet lips on my mouth. I could not help but to push him away and glance deep into his eyes. His eyes told a story his mouth could not speak. We made love that night, like the world was coming to an end. Little did I know that my personal apocalypse was about to take place.

I woke up the next morning, with a shadow over my soul. I rubbed my hands over my belly and felt my angel brush my hand. I never in a million years thought I could love someone this hard. D is my heart and soul, but this child I have been blessed with is the air that flows through my lungs. The clock ticked on the wall and I could feel my pulse beat with every stroke. I sat up and called out to D, "Baby, Baby ….where are you?"

I sat their listening for a response; my ear began to burn as the silence became unbearable. I closed my eyes and prayed as I walked into the living area. I once again called out his name and then noticed him sitting on the deck. The cold paralyzed my hands as I placed my fingers on the freezing glass. I knocked on the sliding glass door, and D turned around and smiled at me. He sat in the cold, with his black goose down coat and toboggan. He seemed to be in a trance as he glared out at the lake in our backyard. D finally stood up and brushed his black Levi's off and entered through the door. I smiled at my King and rubbed his cold ears.

Cursed by the Candy

"Baby, you want something to eat?"

He looked at his watch and said, "Naw, not right now, I am going out for a few. I'm going to take you out tonight when I finish….ok?"

My heart dropped, but I presented a smile for my man. D placed a kiss on my head and turned and walked out the door. The day seemed to go by at a snail's pace, I think I looked at the clock a thousand times waiting for him to walk back through the door. I heard the phone ringing and I paced through the house in search of it. When I finally located it, the ring had stopped. As I turned to walk into the bathroom the phone began to ring again. I picked up the phone and I could hear my D, call my name, "Toi, I need you to come down to the hospital."

My stomach dropped as all kind of madness went through my head. "D….what's wrong? Where are you?"

His voice was a soft whisper, and I heard him say, "My Mom was murdered!" I sat on the floor and searched for words to say. All I wanted to do was get to him NOW.

"Baby what hospital are you at?" I hung up the phone and threw on my clothes, as I locked the front door and pressed the alarm to the car, I could have sworn I saw someone staring at me from across the street. I slowly walked across the snow layered grass and towards the circular driveway and placed my purse in the car. I pulled out of the driveway and saw a black Lexus sitting across the street. I really didn't pay it any attention until I turned a few corners and the vehicle was still trailing behind me. My heart began to beat fast as I approached a rail road crossing. I slowed down and noticed the window rolling down, I turned my head as I saw a black gun come out of the window. I hit the gas and screeched across the tracks. I began to cry and swerved around a corner. I came upon a red light and noticed a police vehicle at the light. I merged to the left of the police car and rolled down my window….as I began to ask for help a man walked aside my car and grabbed my throat; he stared in my face and said, "Tell Don Don, next time I see him, it's over, this is just a warning.

The cop pulled off and never saw a thing.

I began gasping for air as I tried to calm myself down; I heard that voice in the back of my mind, *Toi pull off! Go! D needs you... GO!*

I pressed the gas and flew down the street, by the time I got to the hospital I was a nervous wreck. How could I tell him what happened to me, when his mother was just killed?

As I approached the elevator I could hardly compose myself, my hands were shaking, my stomach hurt. I knew as soon as D saw me he would know something was wrong; I placed my exhausted body in a chair near the elevator and began to pray... "God please help me and my family get through this, I ask you to forgive us all for our sins and place your hands on us."

The tears began to flow down my face and I felt a presence standing over me. I looked up and saw D standing there, looking like a lost child. I stood up and held on to him for dear life; we sobbed in each other's arms. Ours tears flowed for different reasons but the hurt was still the same. My fear of losing him and his heart broken because he just lost his mother. He pushed me away and gently held my chin, "Toi what's going on?" I have never lied to D, the entire time we have been together, but this burden would have to wait, I was here for him right now.

I kissed him on the cheek and said, "I'm okay, just worried about you." As I turned my head I saw a man approaching us in a white coat.

"Excuse me, are you Sandra Miles son?"

D stared at the doctor as though he was an alien and then finally answered him. " Yes, I am ...why?"

The doctor took a breath then said, "I'm sorry for your loss. We did everything we could. I reached for D's hand and gave him a gentle squeeze. The doctor must have sensed his irritation, because he pulled out his pen and told D that he needed him to sign some papers so his mother's belongings could be released.

Cursed by the Candy

D grabbed the pen and scribbled down his signature and dropped the clipboard on the floor. Before I could say anything, D walked away. I looked at the doctor and apologized and trailed behind him. I had so much on my mind I didn't know what to do. However, one thing I did know is I wouldn't be telling him what happened today.

We sat in silence as I rubbed his back softly. No words could take away his pain; I just needed him to know I was there.

~~~~~

It's been two months since D'S Mom died and no one seems to know what happened. There are whispers going around about a drug deal gone wrong, but something in my soul is telling me it's something more.

Every time I look at him I feel like I am betraying him, since I have not found the strength to tell him what happened. The thought of what he will do makes me sick; my baby does not play, and he would blow up all the seven cities if he knew someone threatened our lives.

Our home seems so quiet and lonely. I always thought this is what I wanted, but what's the point when you can't share it with anyone. I keep having dreams about Chanelle. Lawd how I wish I could hug my Momma right now. One thing I do know is that she would never step foot in our home, she already made that very clear. In her words, "I'm not stepping foot in your boyfriend's DRUG PARADISE."

Two months have passed since that awful day and D barely leaves the house. If he does he comes right back. This time has really made me appreciate everything about him, from the smell of his skin to the way he slides his hand through my hair as I sleep. My days are filled with prayers for guidance and strength to get through this last month.

Little D, is definitely making his presence known and I feel like I am the most unattractive woman in the world. I must admit that Desiree has been crossing my mind lately; just as my belly is growing with this gift, she is experiencing the same thing, whether she viewed it as a blessing or not.

My concentration was interrupted as I heard D messing around in the kitchen. I walked around the corner and saw him setting up a scale. I was about to walk away until I heard his voice, "Toi, what's up?" I placed my heavy body against the wall and stared at my King. Before I could get a word out of my mouth I felt a sharp pain penetrate my stomach.

I grabbed the wall for support and bent over. D ran towards me as I began to hit the floor. "Damn, Toi what's wrong?"

The pain began to subside and I placed my hands upon my belly, and said," I think I had a contraction; I sighed and took in a deep breath.

This was the first time I saw D appear to be scared; he pulled me up and held me so tight I could hardly breathe, then I whispered in his ear ,"Baby, I'm ok this is a part of the process".

He looked at me and said, "The HELL with the process you scared the shit outa me."

We slowly walked into our bedroom and sat on the bed. I reached over and grabbed a bottle of water off of the nightstand. I could feel D staring at me from the corner of my eye and I knew I had to be strong for the both of us. I slowly turned around and caressed his hand, "Babe would you mind running me a bath? I think it will help with the pain."

D looked at me strange and said, "Toi what a bath going to do? We need to go to the hospital!" I had read enough books to know that this was just my body getting prepared for the real ordeal. I smiled at him and tried my hardest to make him feel confident, and asked him again to run me a bath.

"D, I'm good I just want to take a bath." He took a deep breath and went toward the bathroom, I must admit I was scared to death and was praying that the pain I was feeling was nothing but my body getting ready for Little D to make his appearance.

Chapter 9

D was taking forever to run my water, so I walked into the bathroom and saw him sitting on the side of the tub, he was in such a deep trance, he did not even see me standing there.

"What's going on, are you ok?"

He looked up at me and said, "Toi, something ain't right, I can feel it all in my soul, ever since my Momma died, I been feeling straight up paranoid. That's why I don't ever leave this damn house; I swear if something happened to you and the baby, I will lose my fucking mind!" A chill went down my spine as I heard the words flow out his mouth. As I was about to confess to him everything that happened that night, an overwhelming feeling of nausea came over me. I ran towards the toilet and threw up, most of it made it in, but the rest dripped down the side. I held on to the toilet as the tears ran down my face. I looked towards D and said, "I really need that bath now".

D, walked out the bathroom and allowed me a moment to get myself together; he made it a point to leave the door opened and told me to holler if I needed him. Never in a million years did I think I would need him so soon.

One minute I was rubbing my belly and the next I was sitting in a river of blood!

I screamed as loud as I could ….. "D, COME HERE!" I was so scared, I tried to jump out of the bath and almost fell over the side of the bathtub. I grabbed ahold of the shower curtain and D caught me just in time.

"What the hell is going on? DAMN WHAT HAPPENED!?"

I screamed, "Baby lay me down and call the ambulance now! I think the baby is coming."

D scrambled to lay me down and ran out the room looking for the phone. I watched him run out when another sharp pain penetrated my body, "OWWWWWWWW, HELPPPPPP, D."

As he approached the door I could feel my baby's head in between my thighs. I screamed for D to help me.

"The baby is coming now D...like right now!"

He grabbed my legs and pulled them apart and the look of horror on his face I will never forget. He looked so helpless, all he could say is, "What am I supposed to do?"

Right then, I felt the urge to push and I did as hard as I could, and baby D, landed in his daddy's arms.

D held our son as the fluids poured through his fingertips and the cord hung between my legs. I struggled to breath and then I heard the sweetest sound ever… it was my baby crying….our baby taking his first breath in this world.

I struggled to sit up and look at this creation we were blessed with, when I felt another gush of blood.

"D something's wrong."

He laid the baby down and looked below my legs and said, "Oh shit, Toi there is so much blood."

He jumped up and called 911.

All I could see was white and I felt so cold; I could hear the baby screaming and D talking, but I could not move. It seemed like forever and then I heard the doorbell ring. D kissed my head and said he would be right back.

I continued to go in and out of consciousness until I heard a loud pop sound then two more. I opened my eyes and saw this man standing over me with a gun. He smiled at me and said … "This is for Desiree"……

Pa-pop, pop, pop.

~~~~~

GOD….I hope the Candy is sweeter on the other side.

Cursed by the Candy

Thanks for reading "*Cursed by the Candy*"; the 1st release from KaToi Love. We really appreciate your support; please be sure to leave a review and remember to tell a friend. You may also read more titles from PRINTHOUSE BOOKS Author's. All titles are available anywhere that books are sold and reviews can be read on participating websites.

KaToi Love

PRINTHOUSE BOOKS

Read it, Enjoy it, Tell a Friend!

Atlanta, Ga.

www.Printhousebooks.com

www.ingramcontent.com/pod-product-compliance
Lightning Source LLC
Chambersburg PA
CBHW031419150426
43191CB00006B/322